AF378588

THE
POOL

Iain Sarjeant

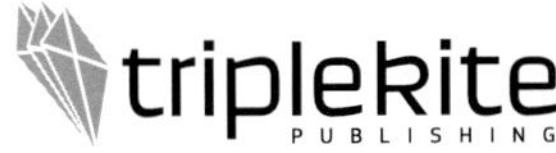

First Published 2014

Photography copyright © 2014 Iain Sarjeant. Text copyright @21014 Wayne Ford.

A catalogue record for this book is available from the British Library.

ISBN 978-0-9576345-6-5

Designed by Dav Thomas. Printed in Malta

Foreword

Within a small Highland woodland near the rural village of Strathpeffer, a pool of still crystal clear water sits silently; its mirror like surface occasionally shimmering in the breeze, its gently sloping banks fringed with a myriad of ferns and grasses, and the air full of the marvellous melodies of bird song, the rustle of leaves and the occasional creek of a branch.

This little pool – that measures no more than two metres in diameter – is the beating heart, the life source of the woodland. Yet, whilst finches and tits drop down for an occasional sip of its waters, and insects skate across its surface that is dappled in light and shadow like some theatrical stage, the pool – the inner sanctum – goes largely unnoticed by those who live nearby, shielded from any undeserving eyes by an honour guard of silver birch.

But from time-to-time someone passes-by – maybe a villager taking their pet dog for an evening stroll, a jogger or a cyclist – who is able to see and appreciate the beauty of this spot. And for a few minutes they may stop and gaze upon this small oasis of wonder, slowly deciphering the complex layers of light and shadow that dances upon the waters surface; with their time being amply rewarded as the pool slowly shares a few, but not all of its secrets and wonders.

Iain Sarjeant is one of those few.

In his subtle and at times almost abstract images Iain does not offer the viewer an all encompassing view of the pool, instead he opts to focus on delicate details in a series of visual notes that come together in an orchestrated whole as an intimate portrait of the pool. However, like the place itself Iain's sensual images never fully reveal themselves on a single visit, each choosing to hold something back that invites the viewer to return from time-to-time like the place itself; and with each visit, these exquisite images reveal something new or previously unseen – a blade of grass, a ripple of water, a leaf – something of such simplicity, that one can only marvel at the richness and beauty to be found in and around the pool.

Wayne Ford

For Iona

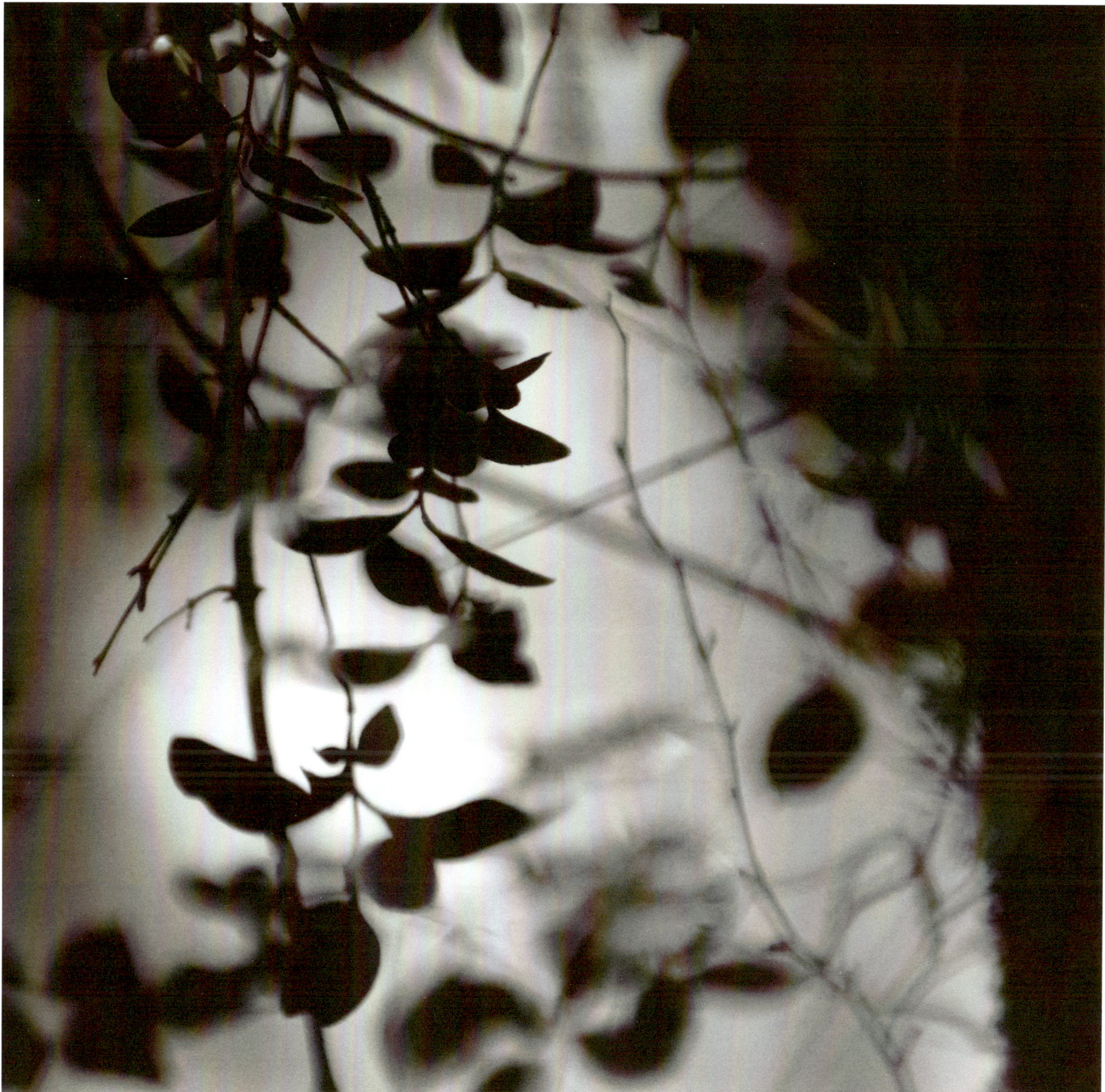

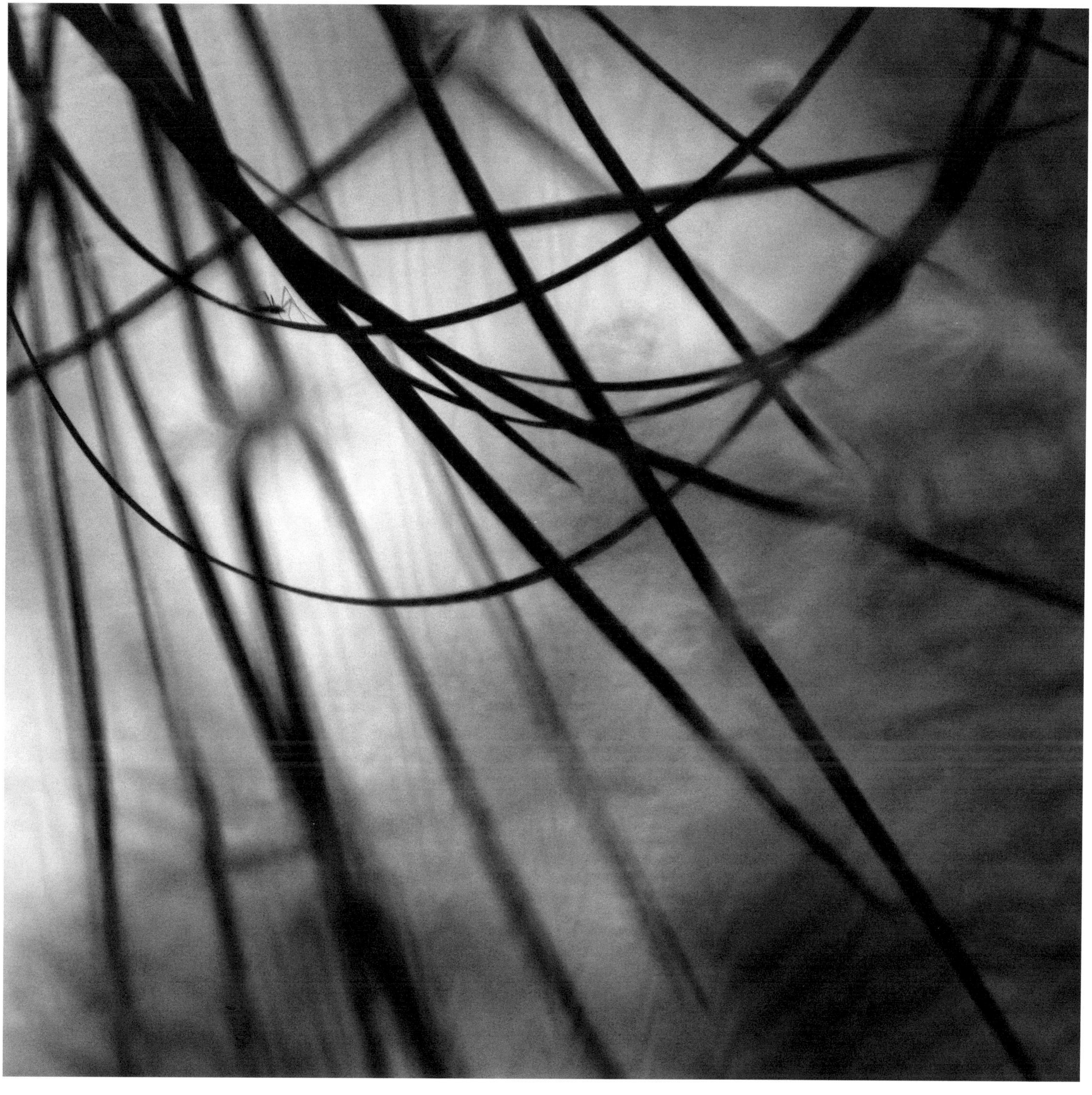

12

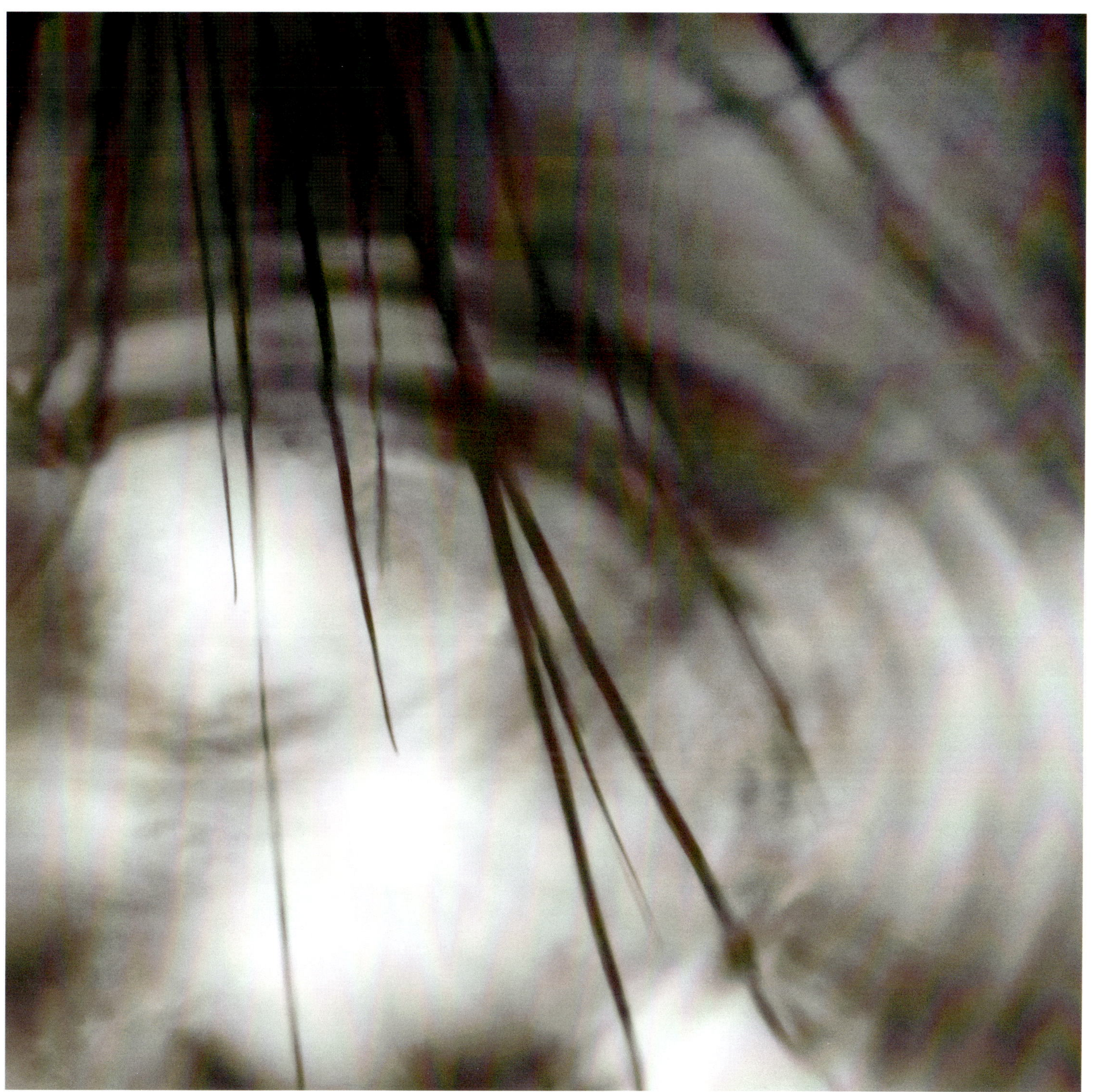

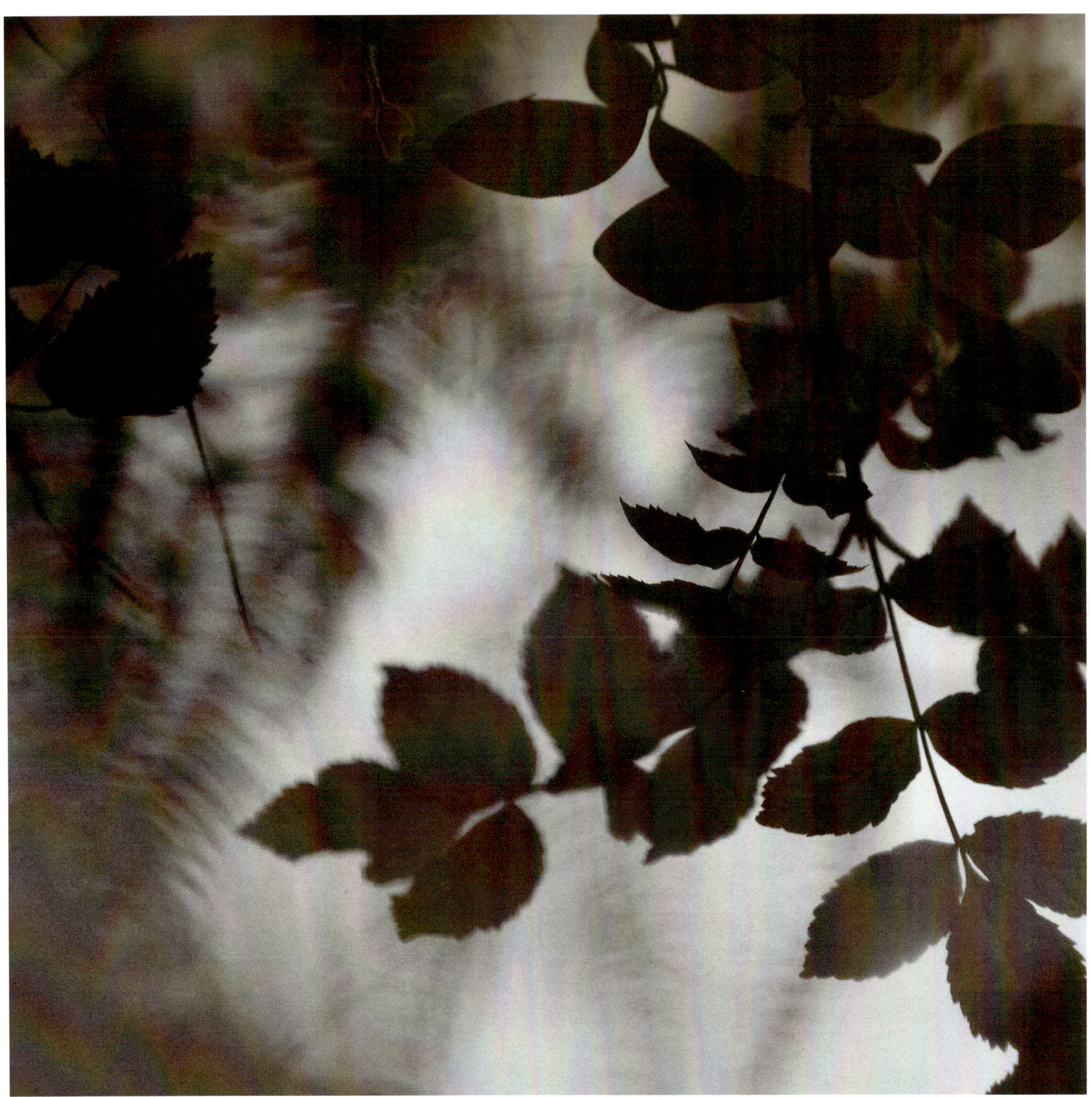

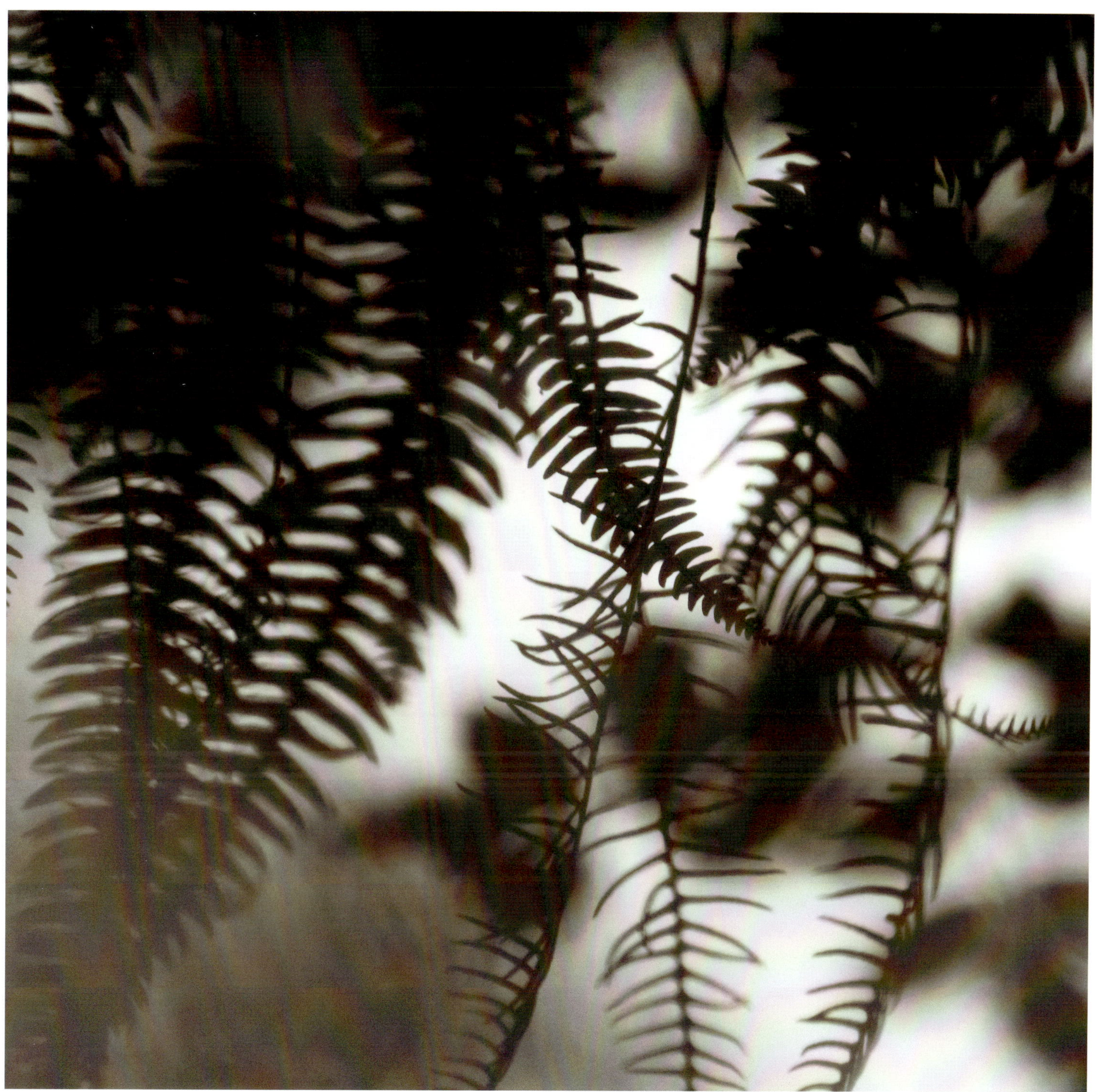

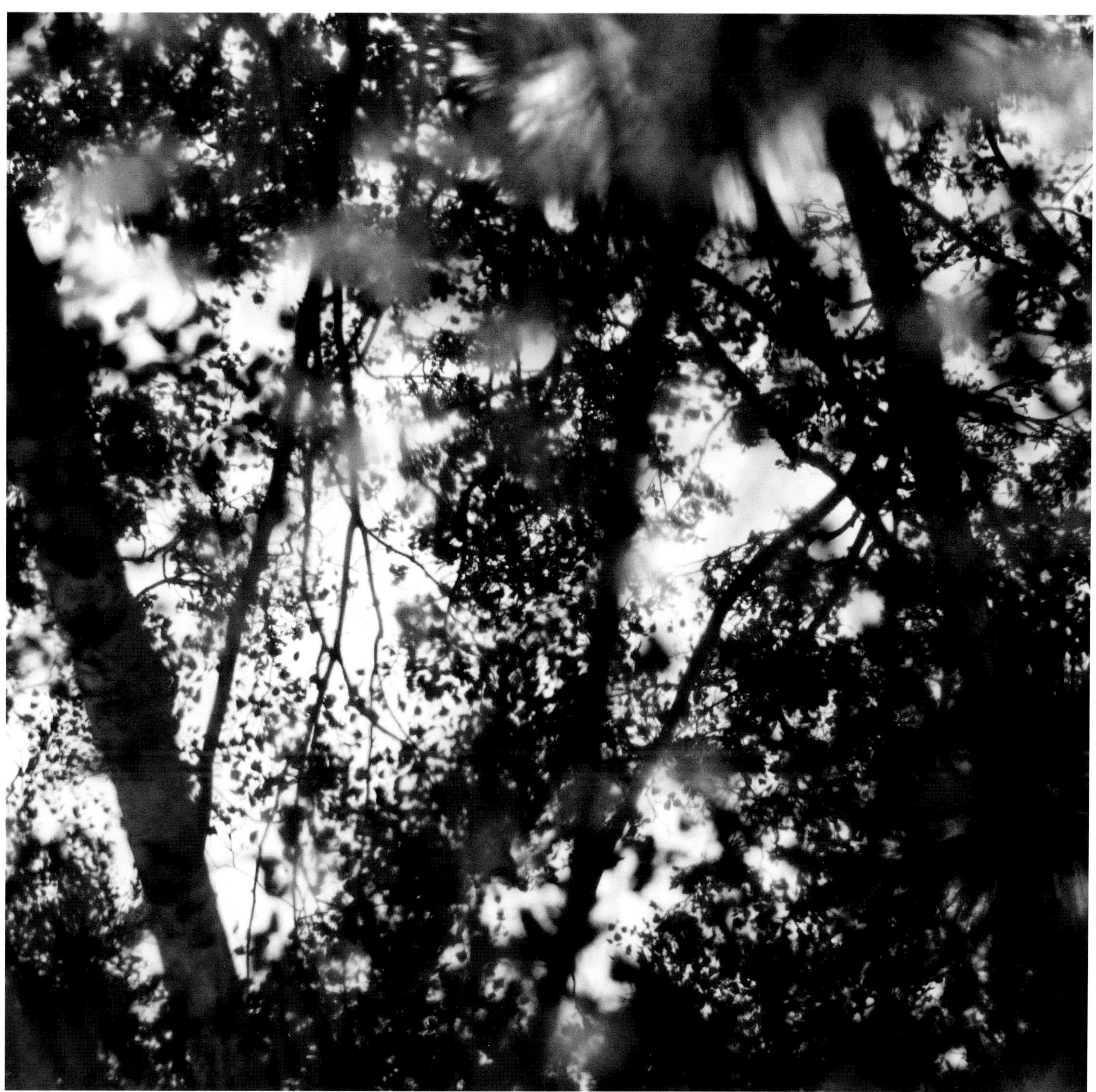

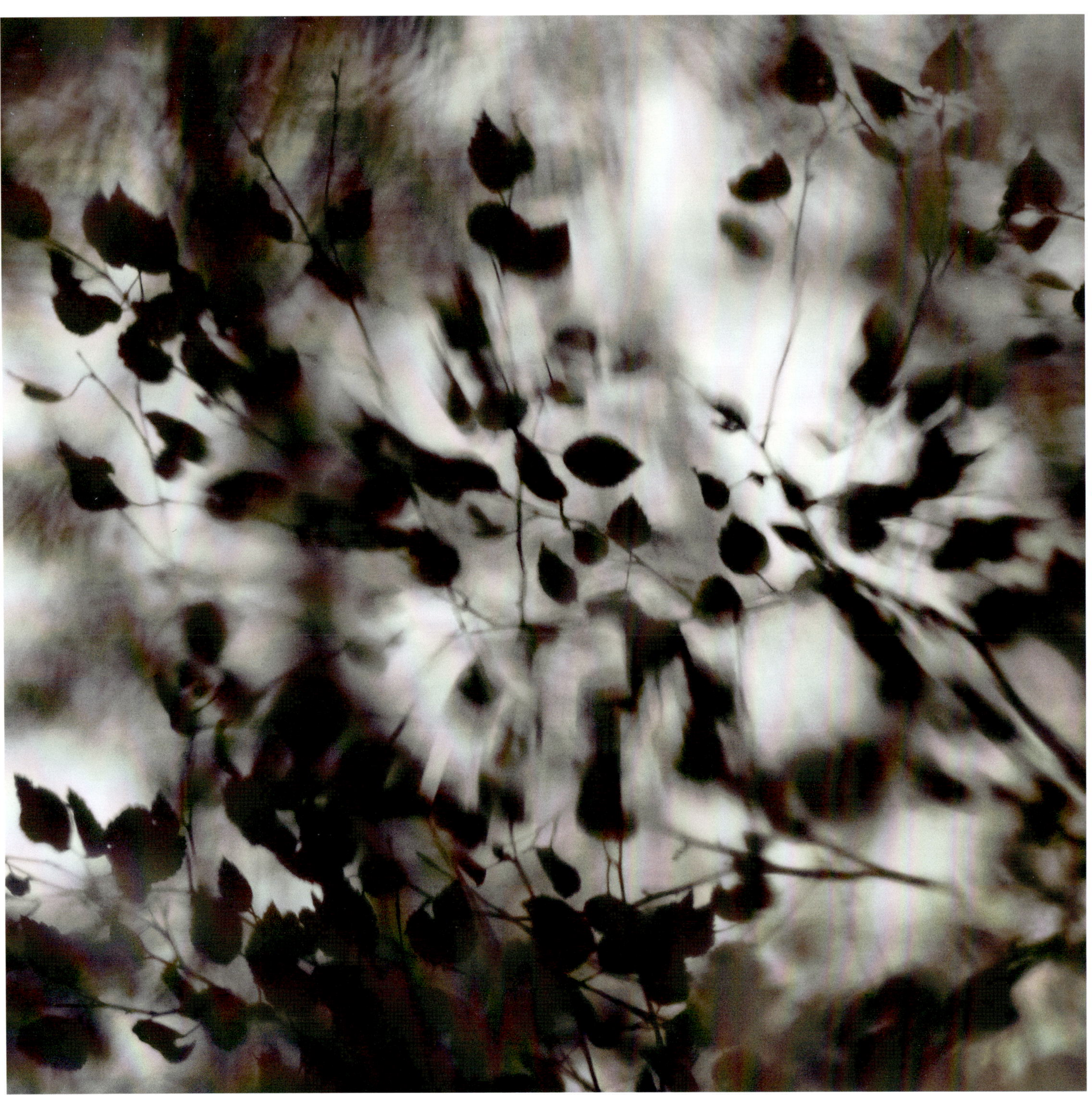

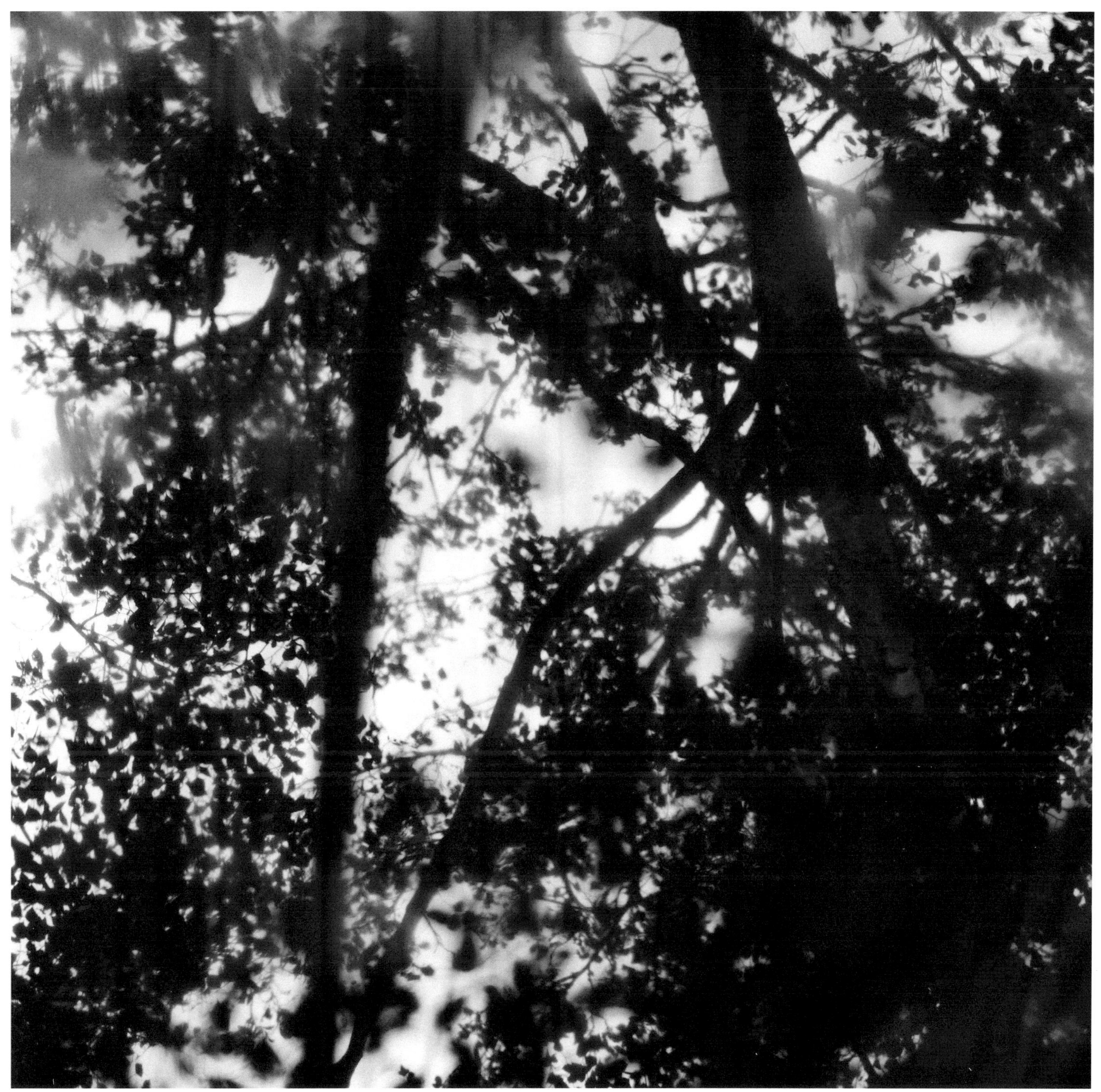

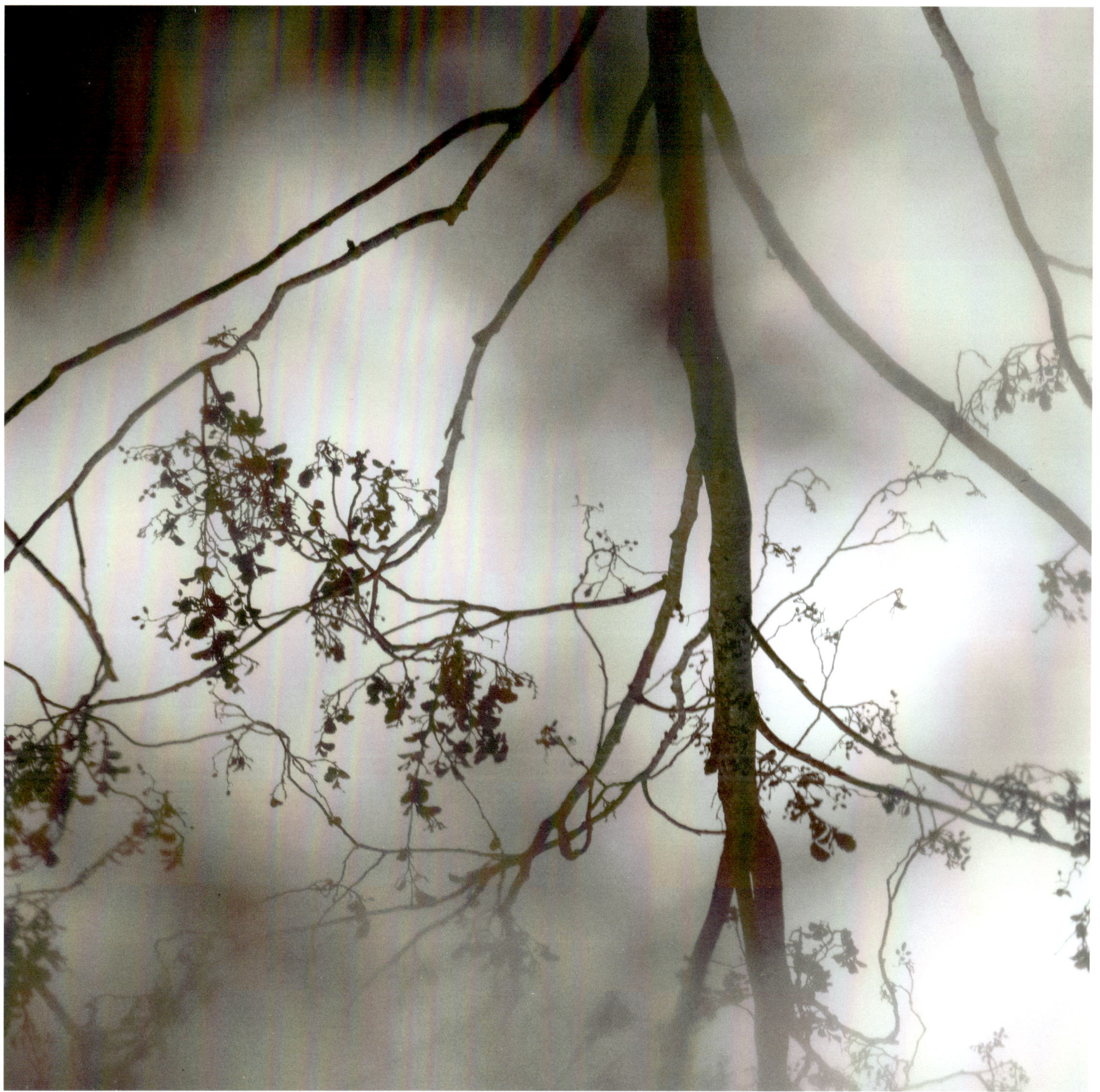

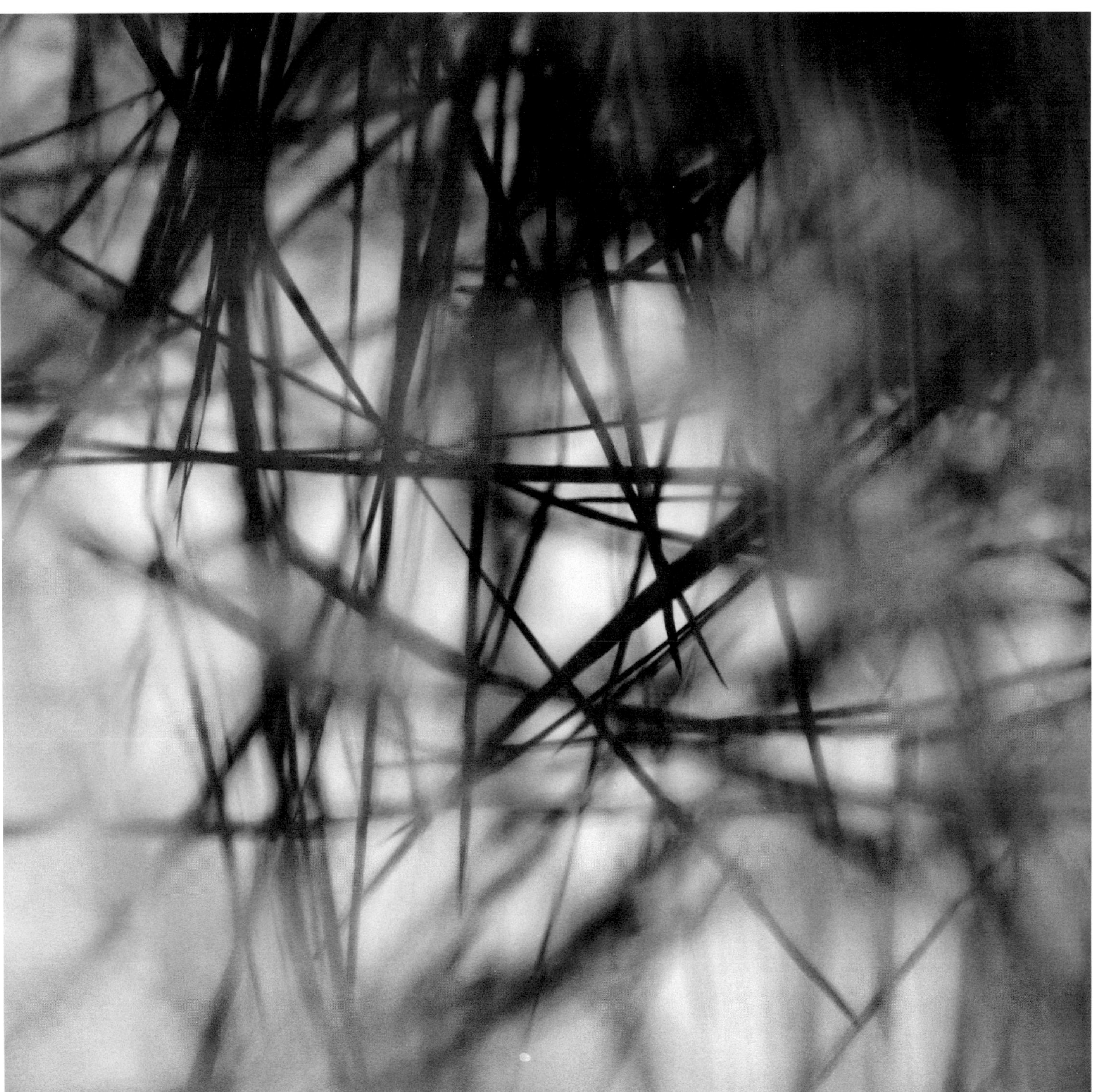

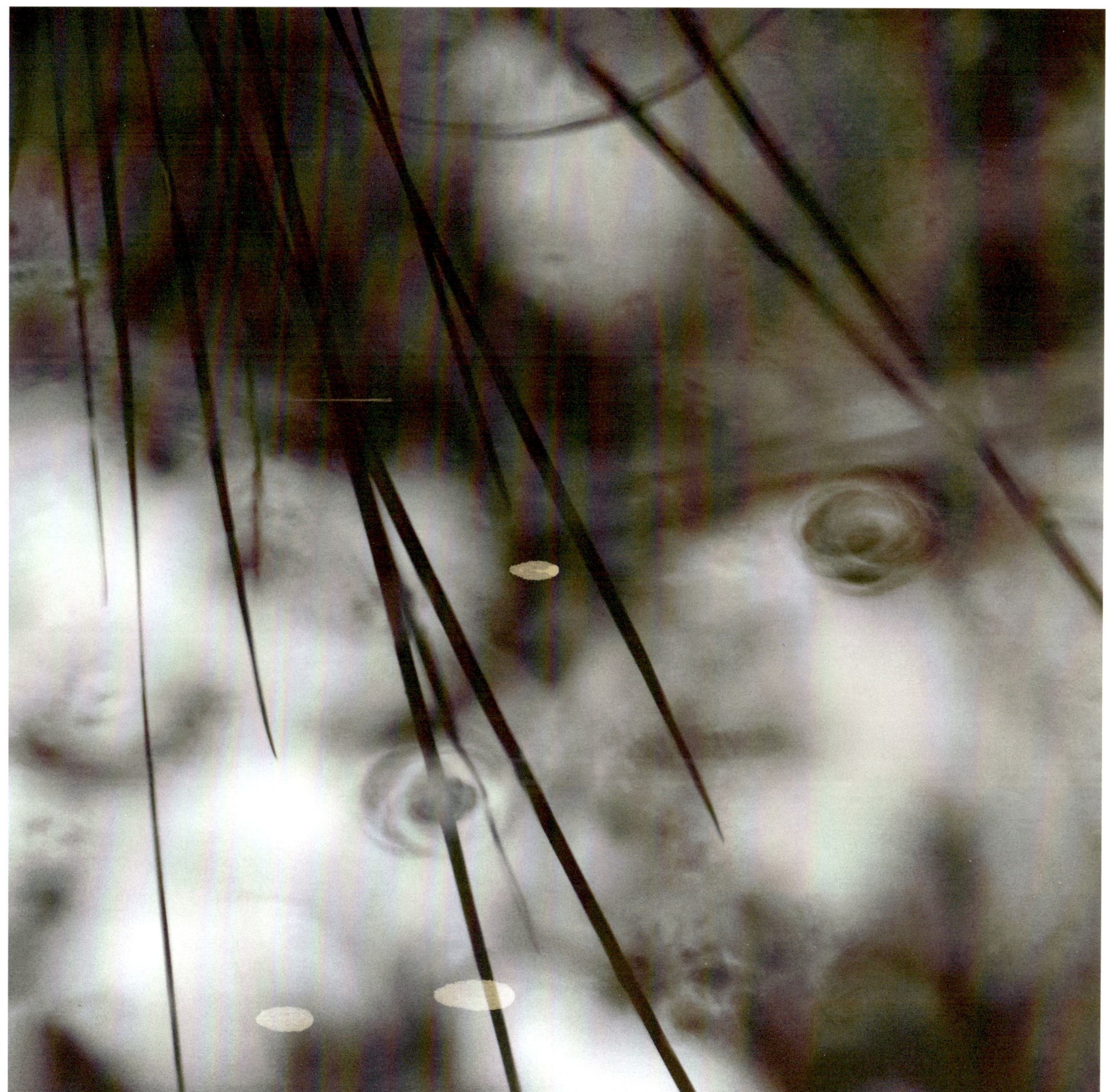

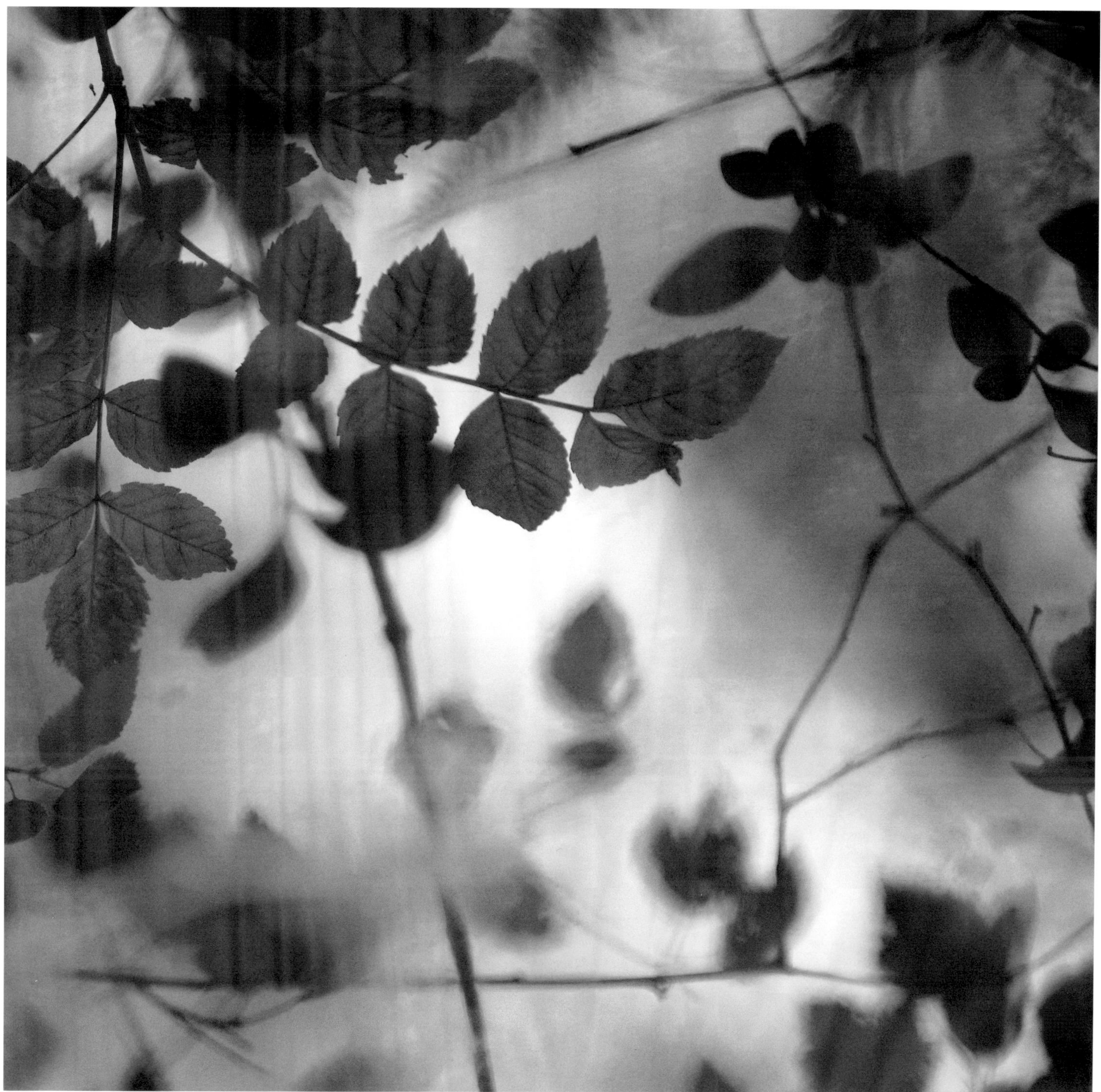

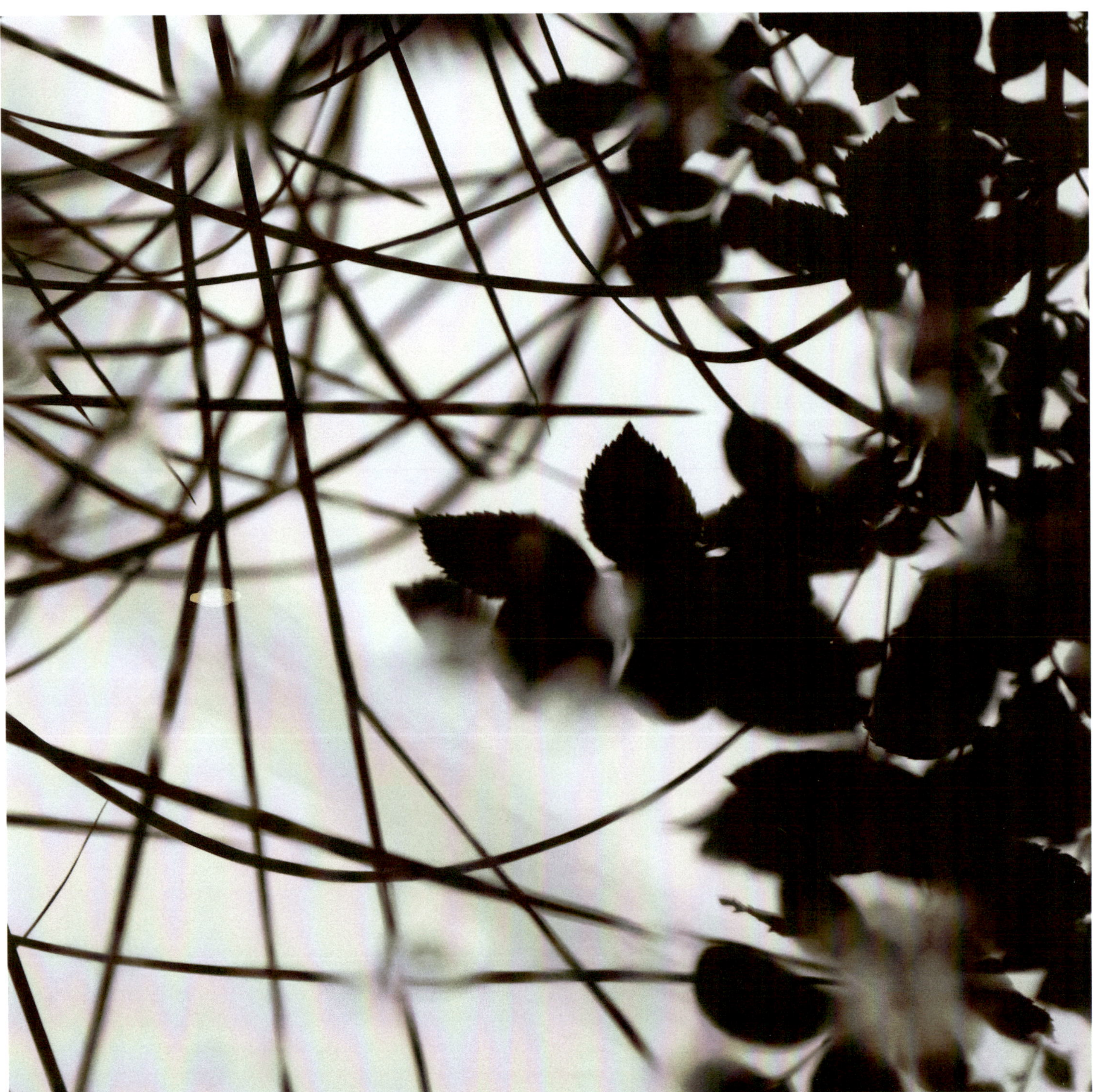

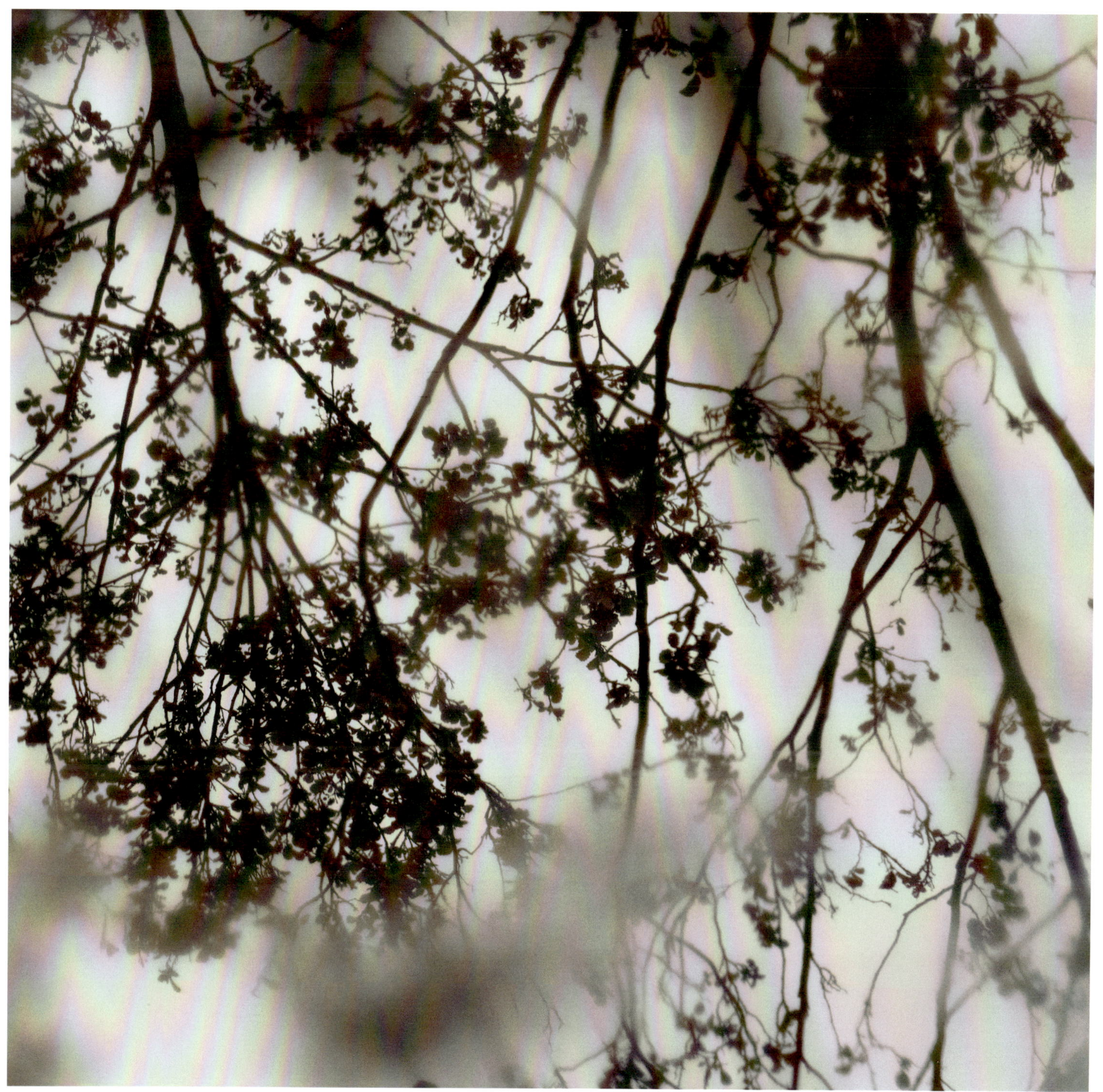

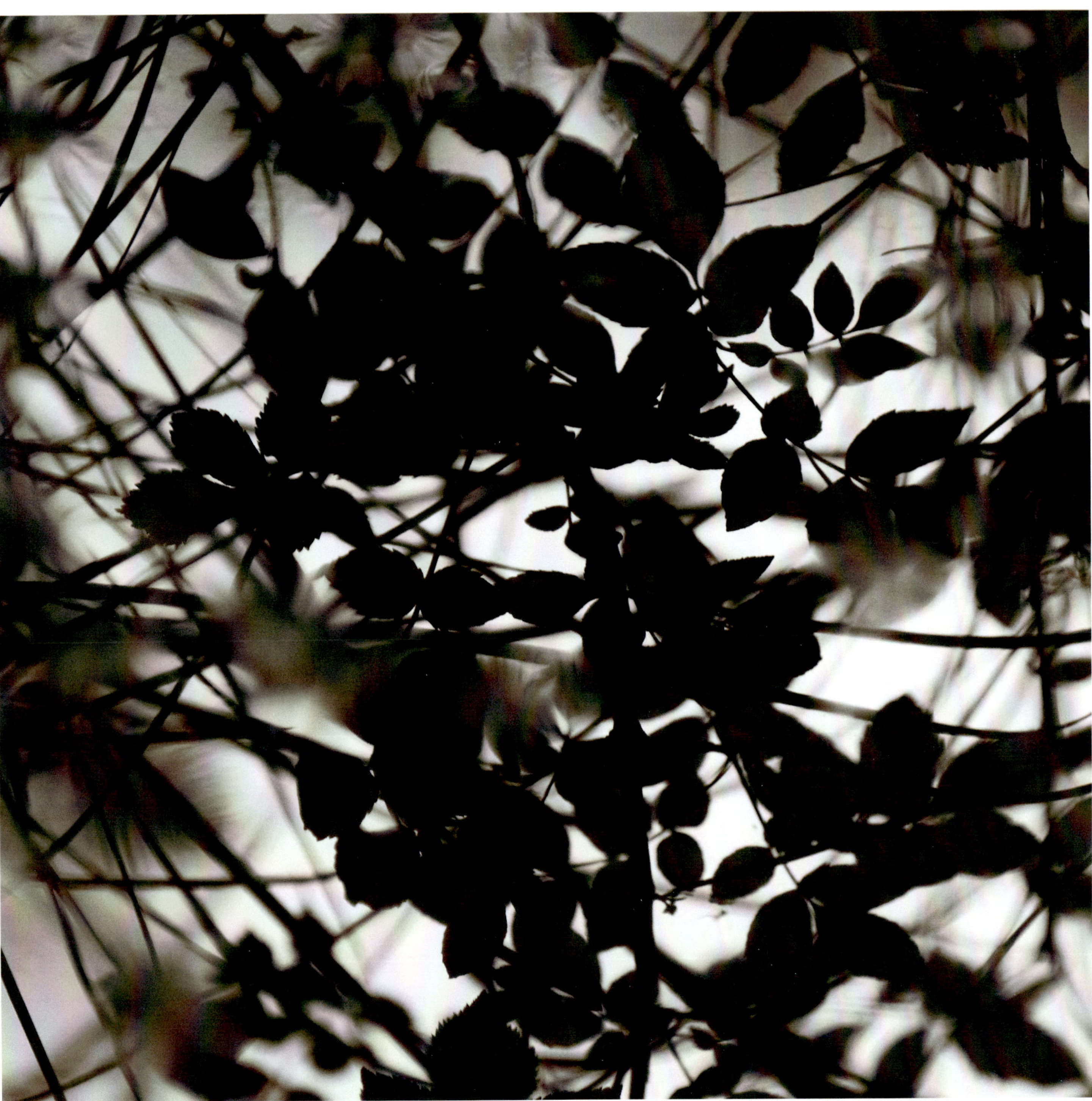

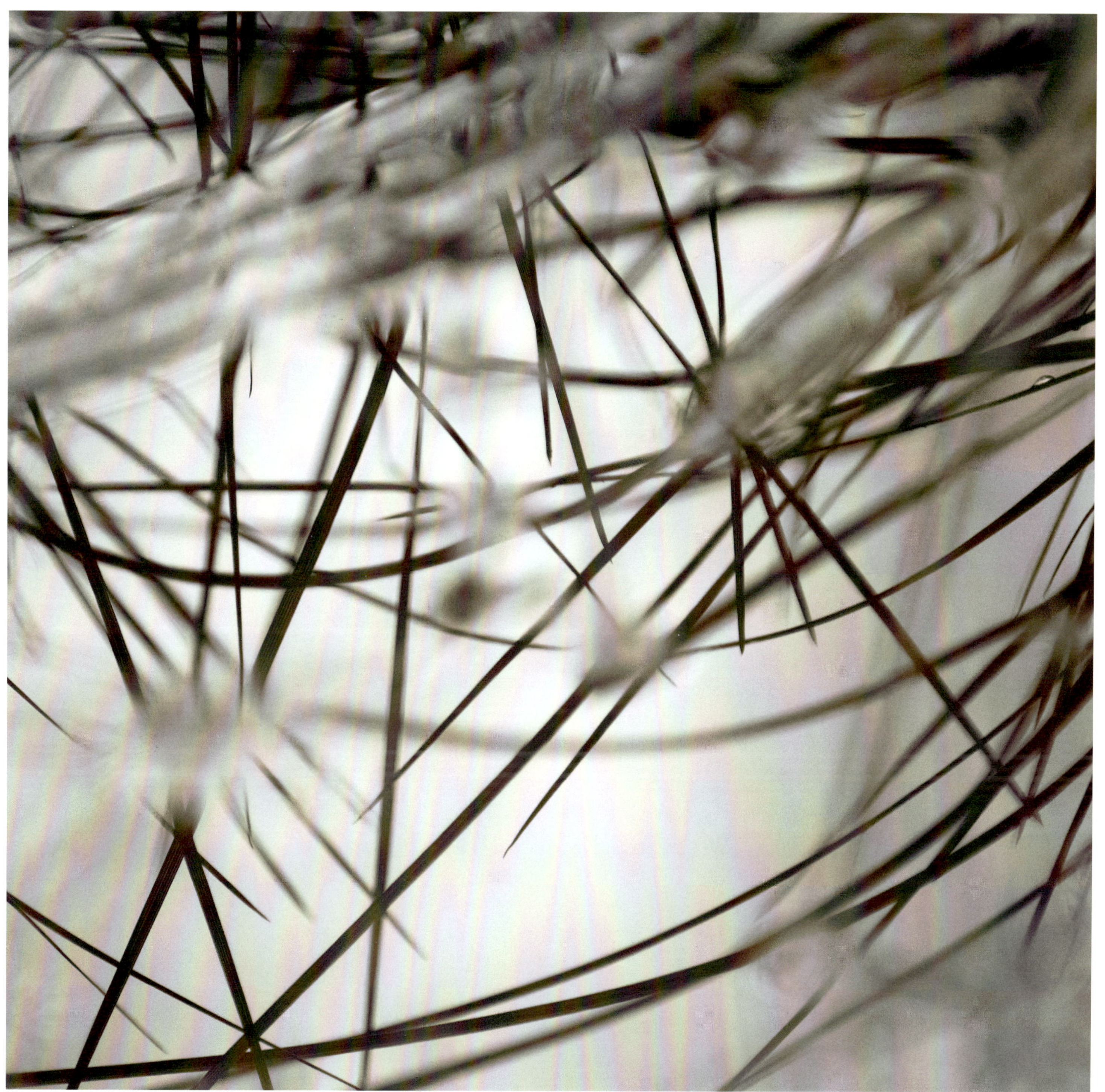

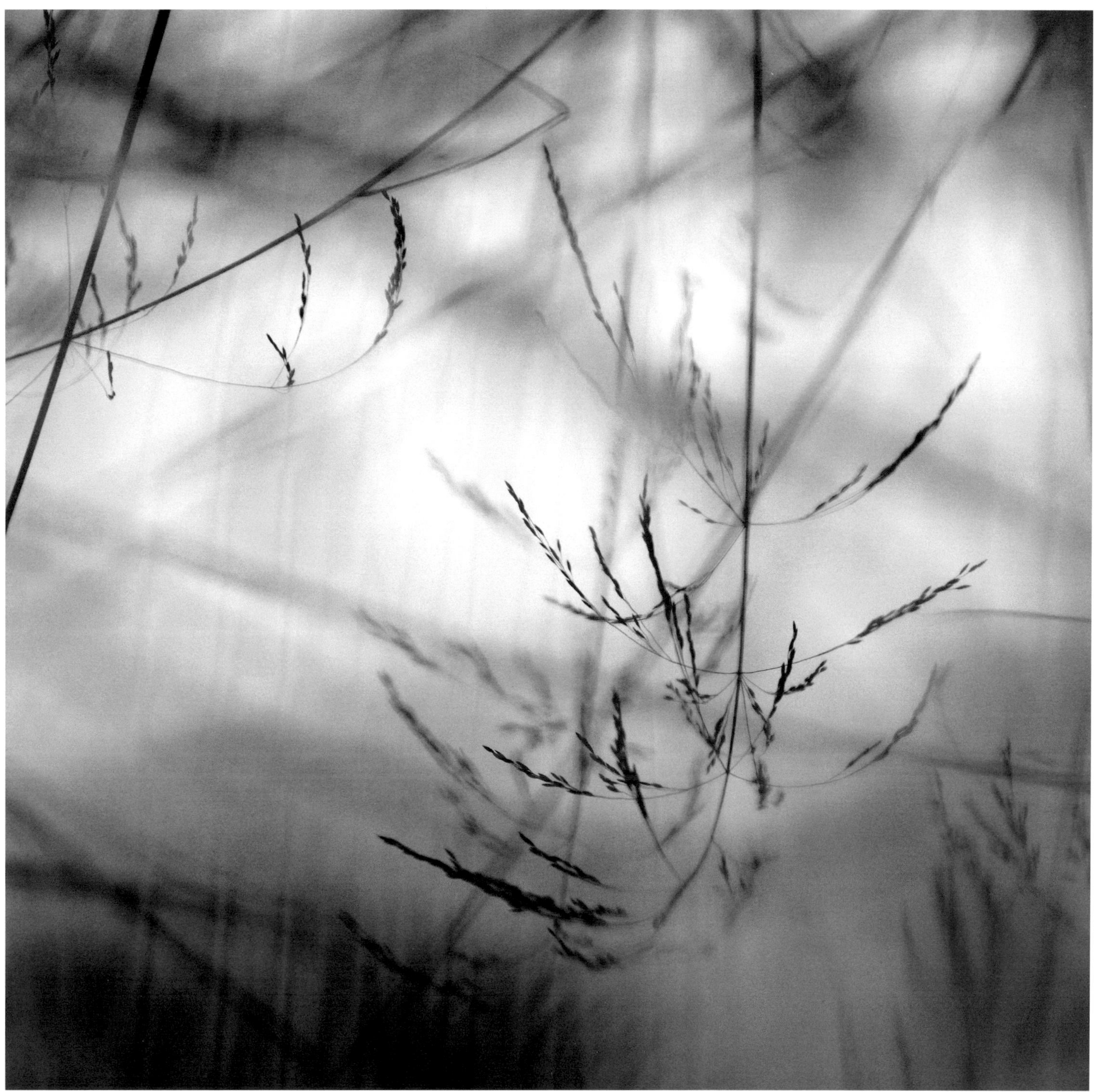

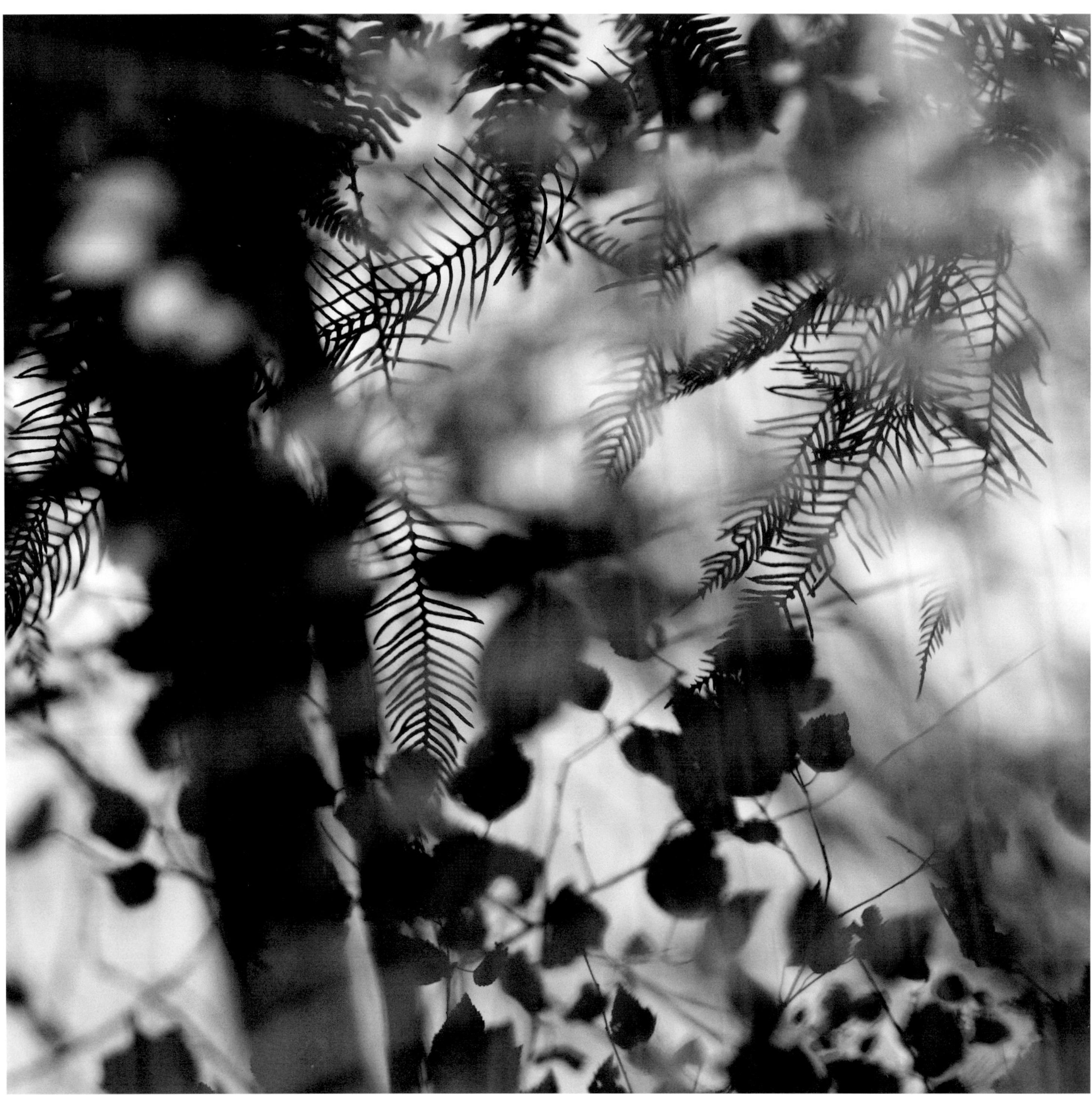

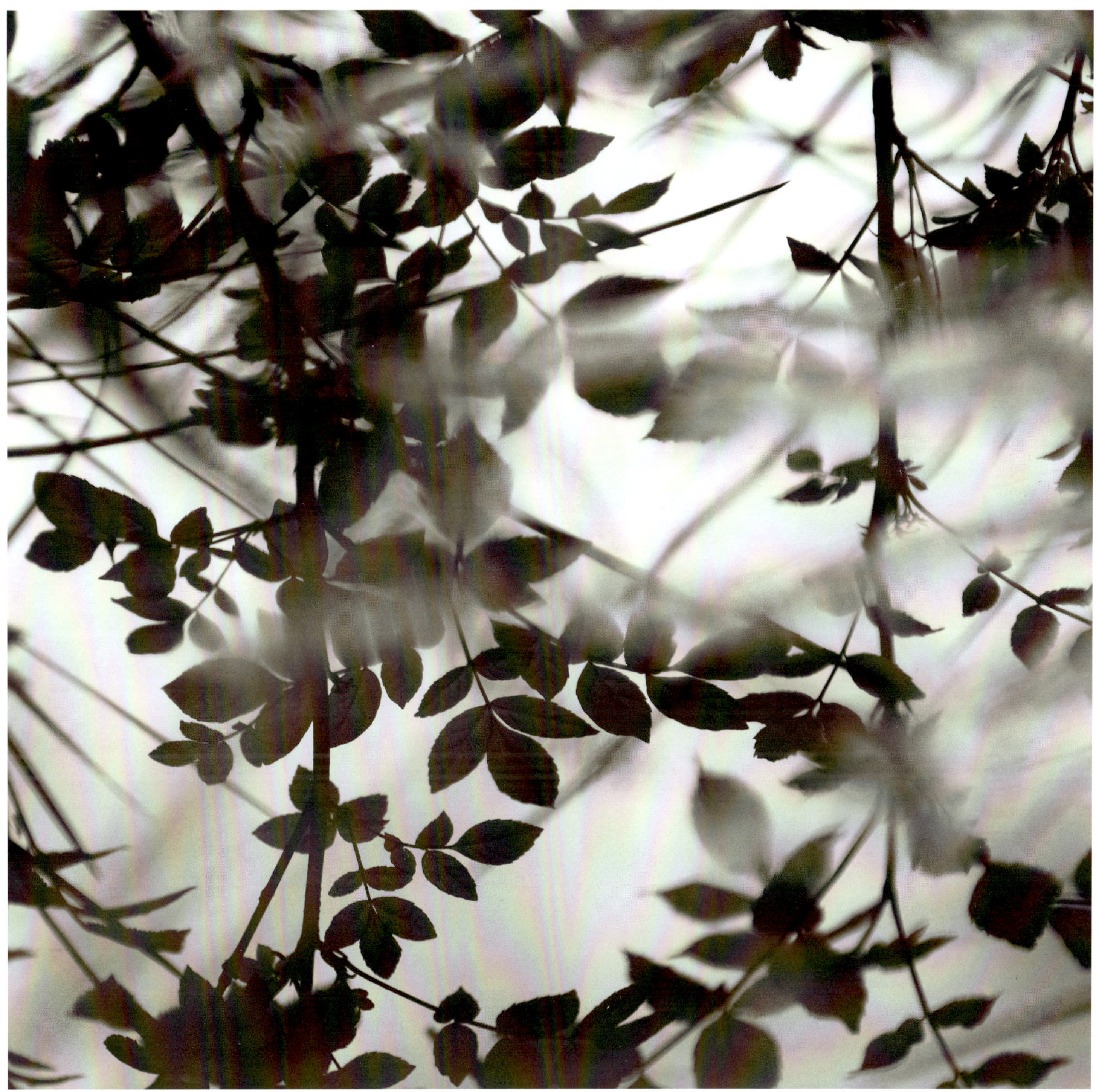

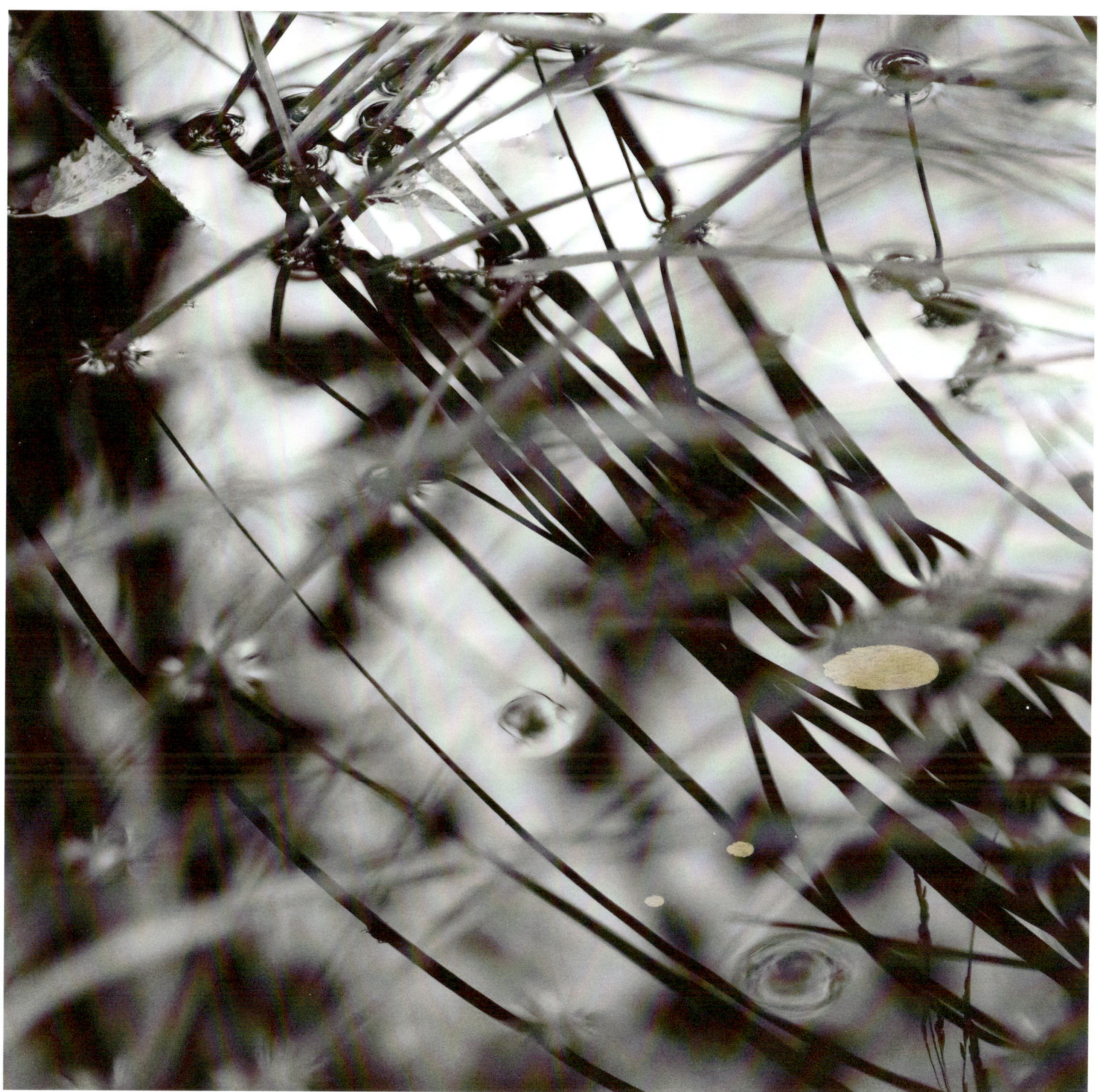

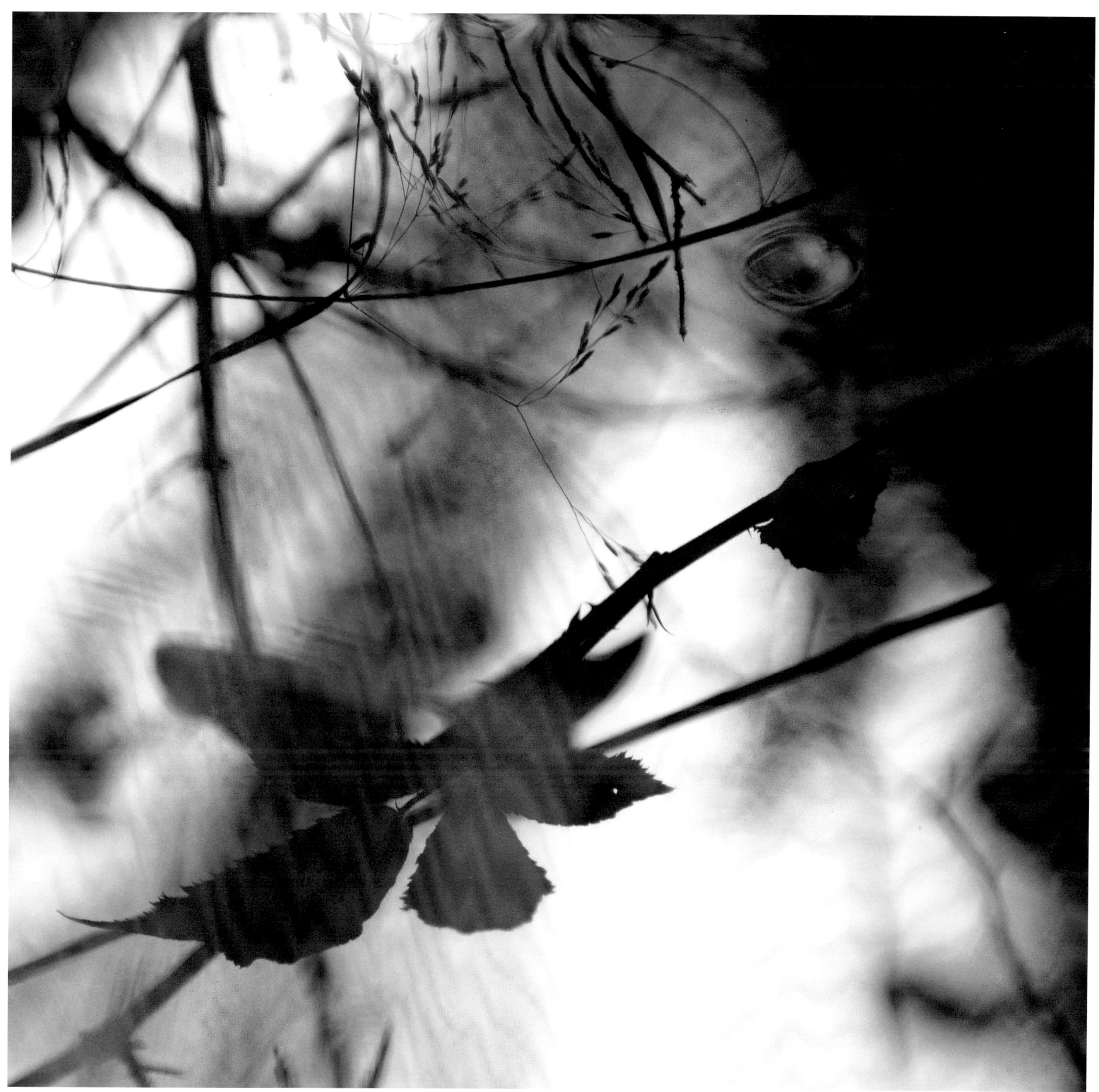

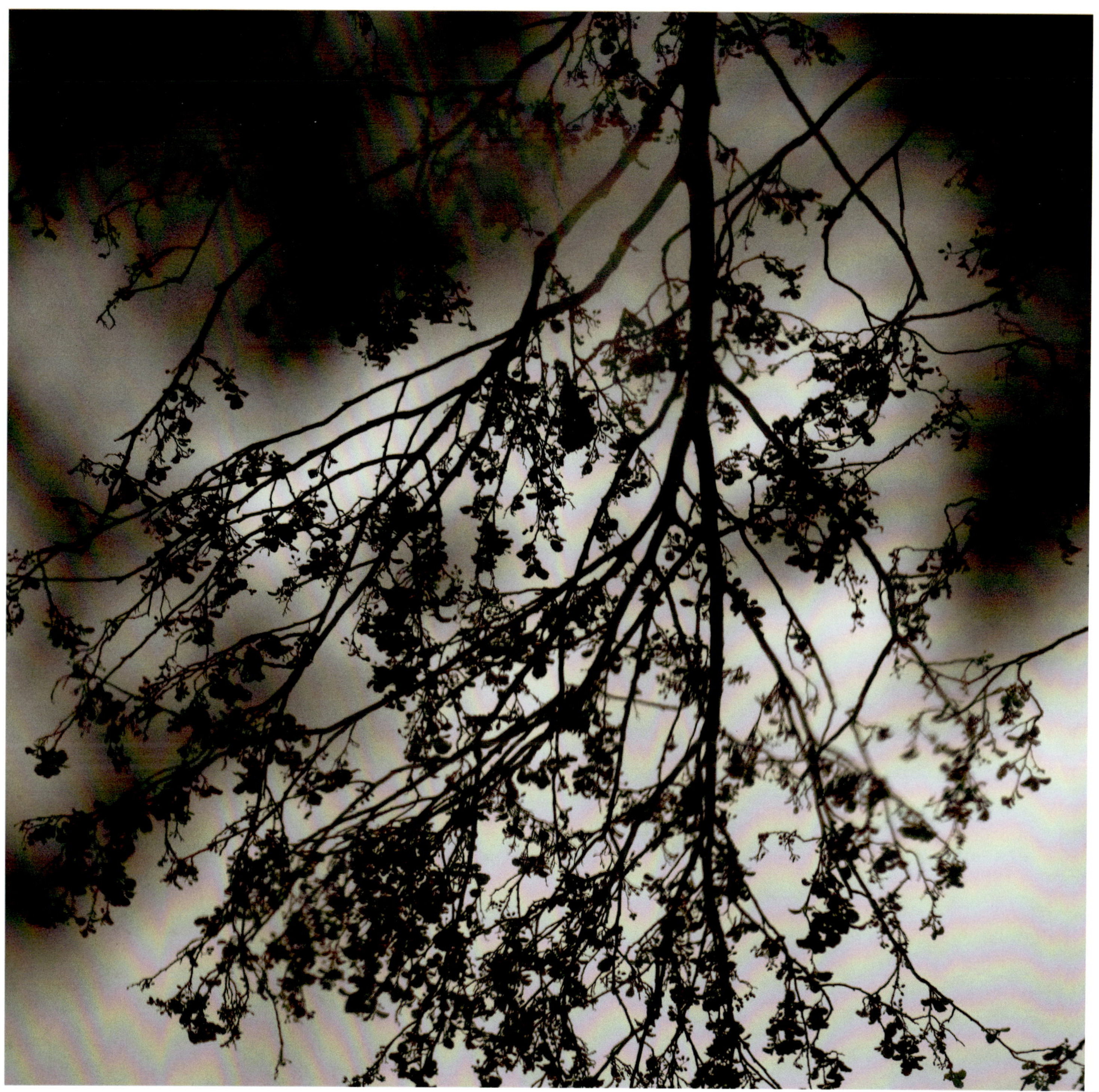

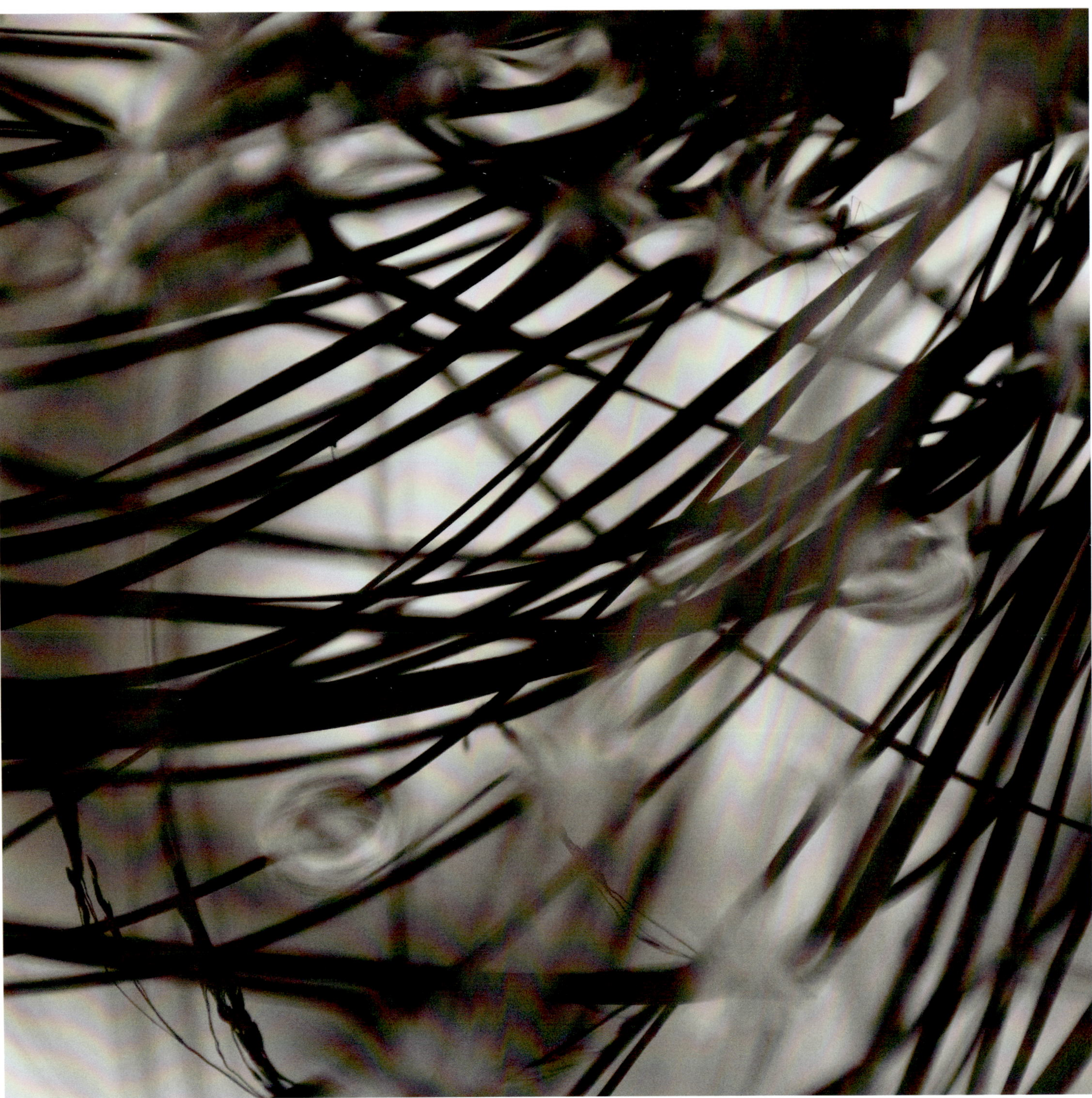

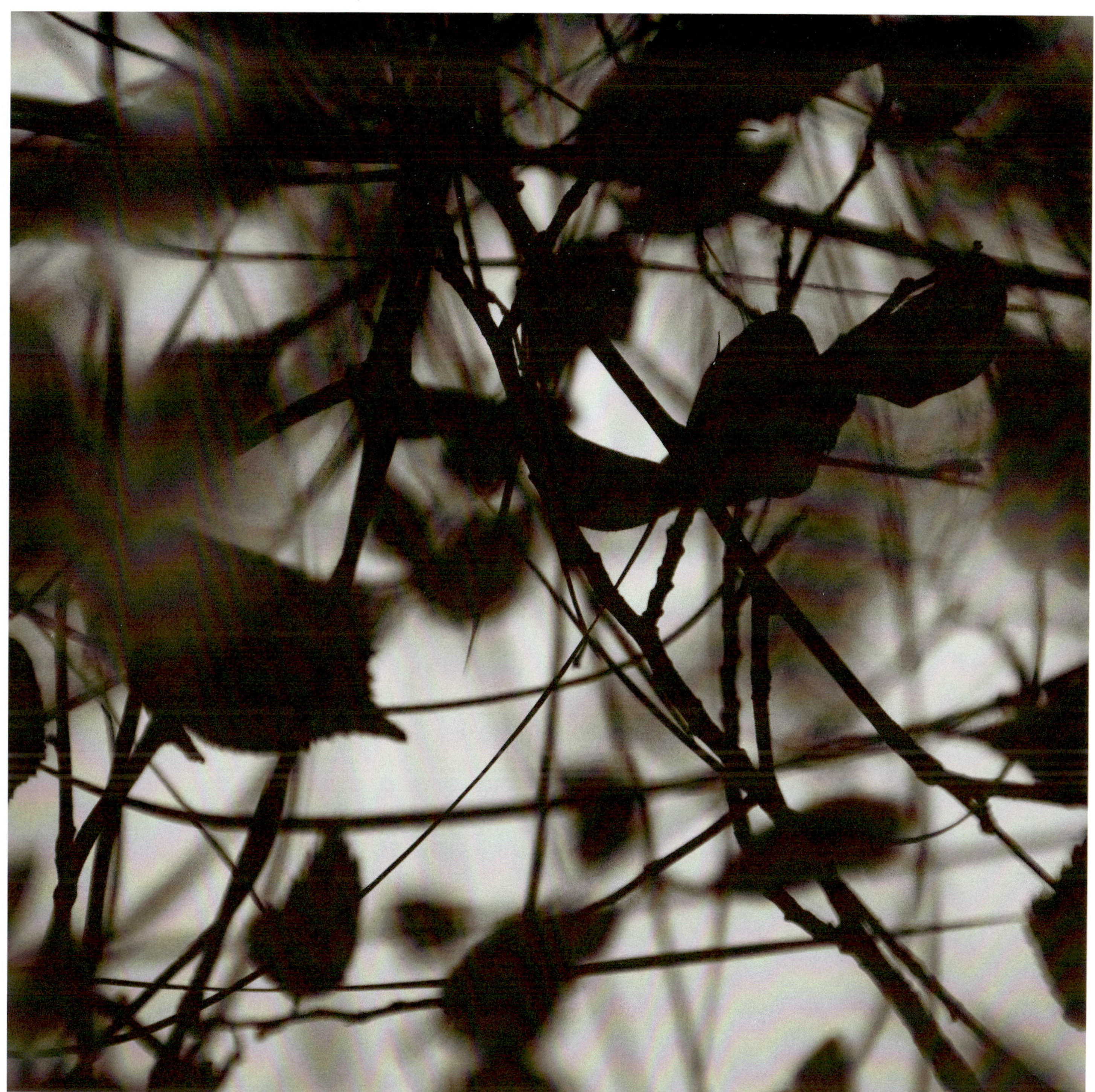

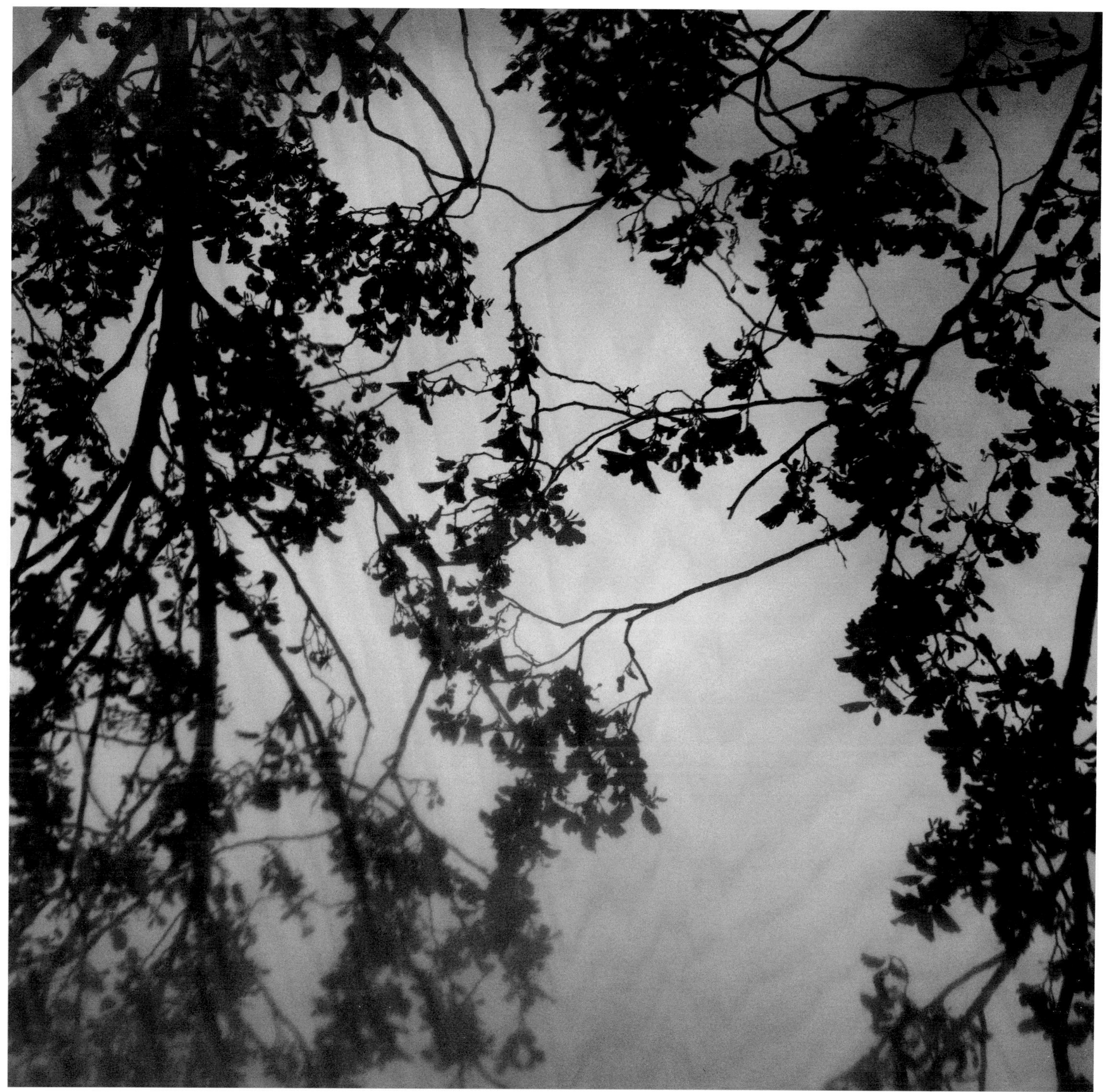

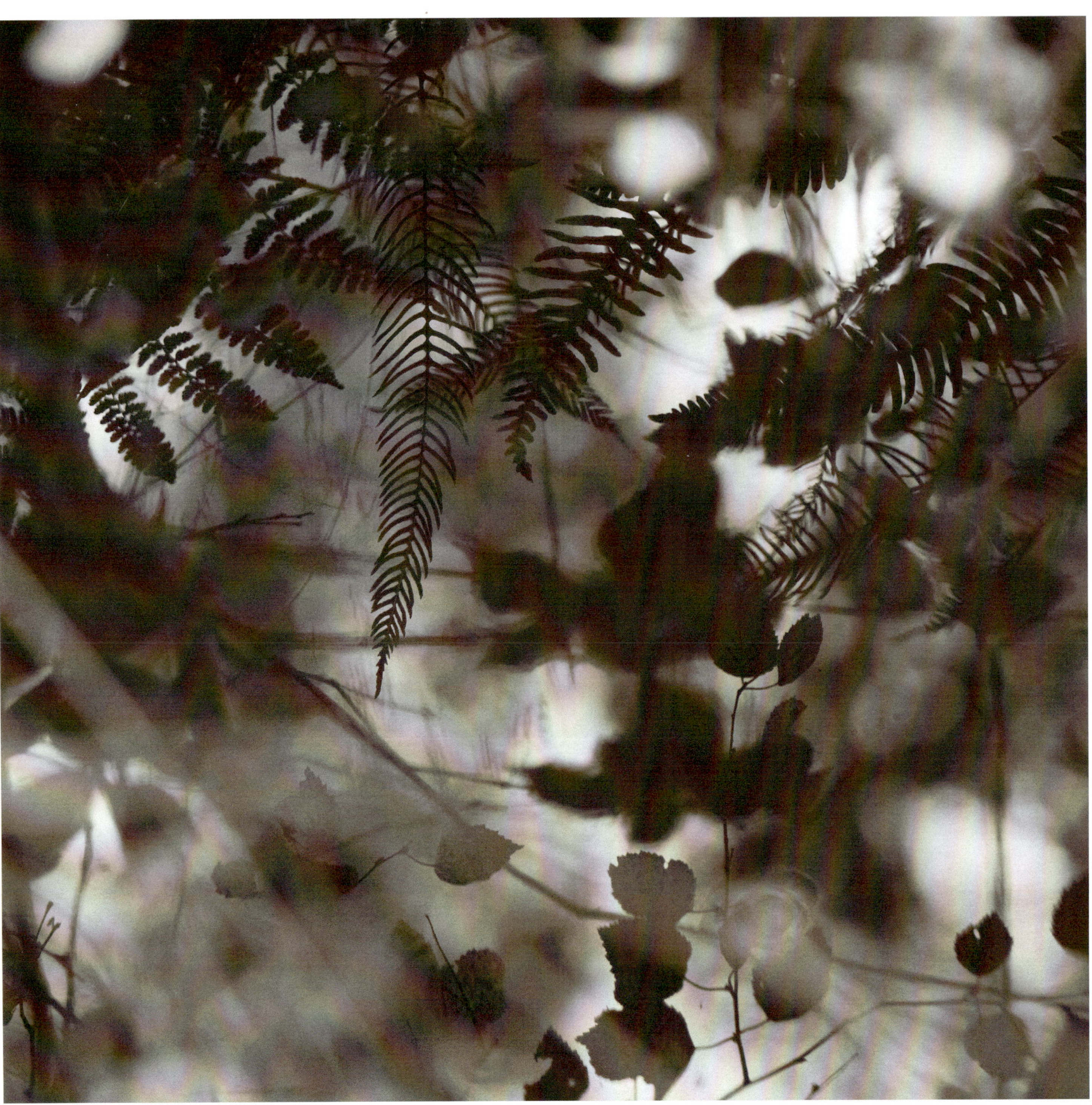

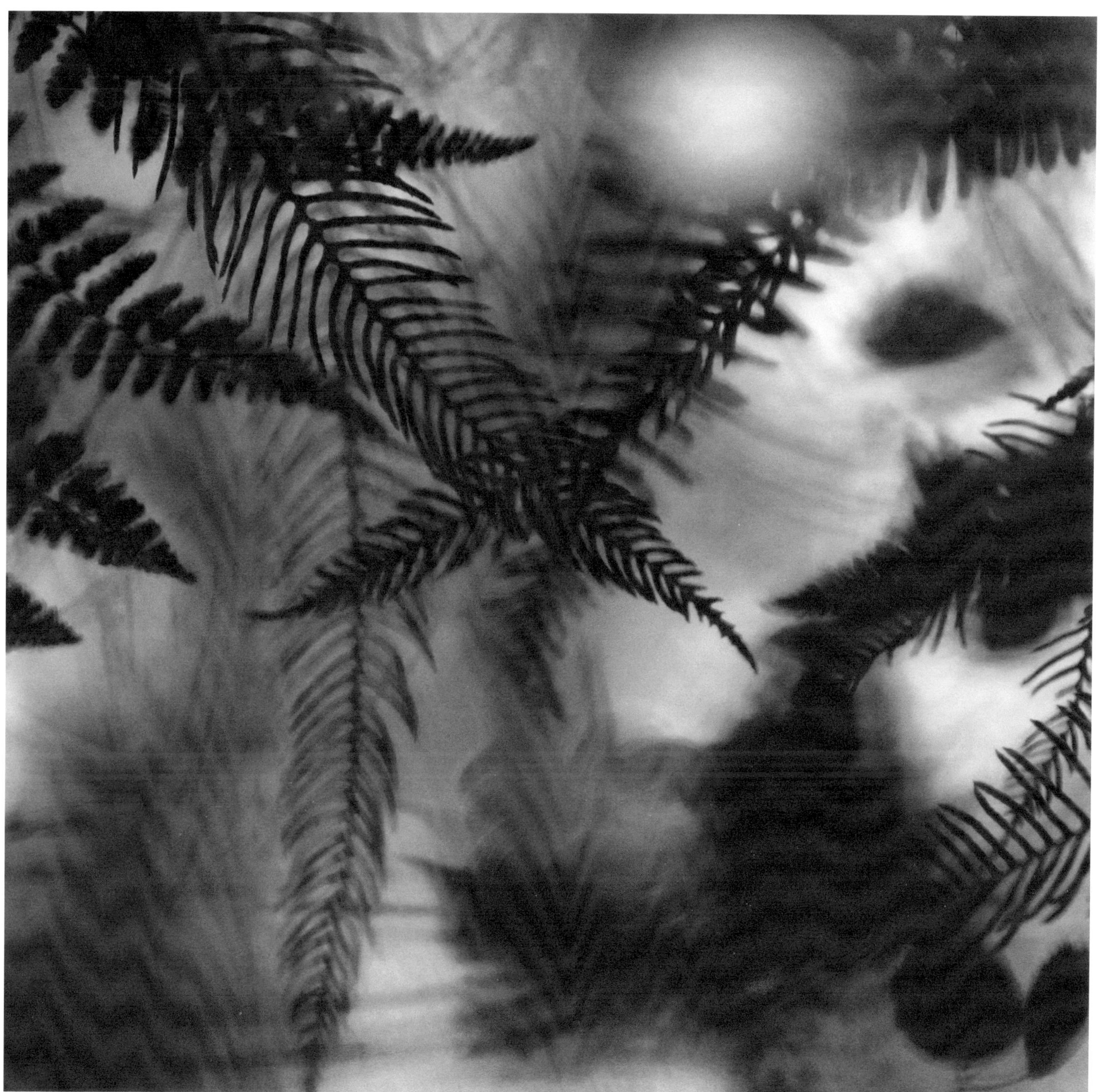

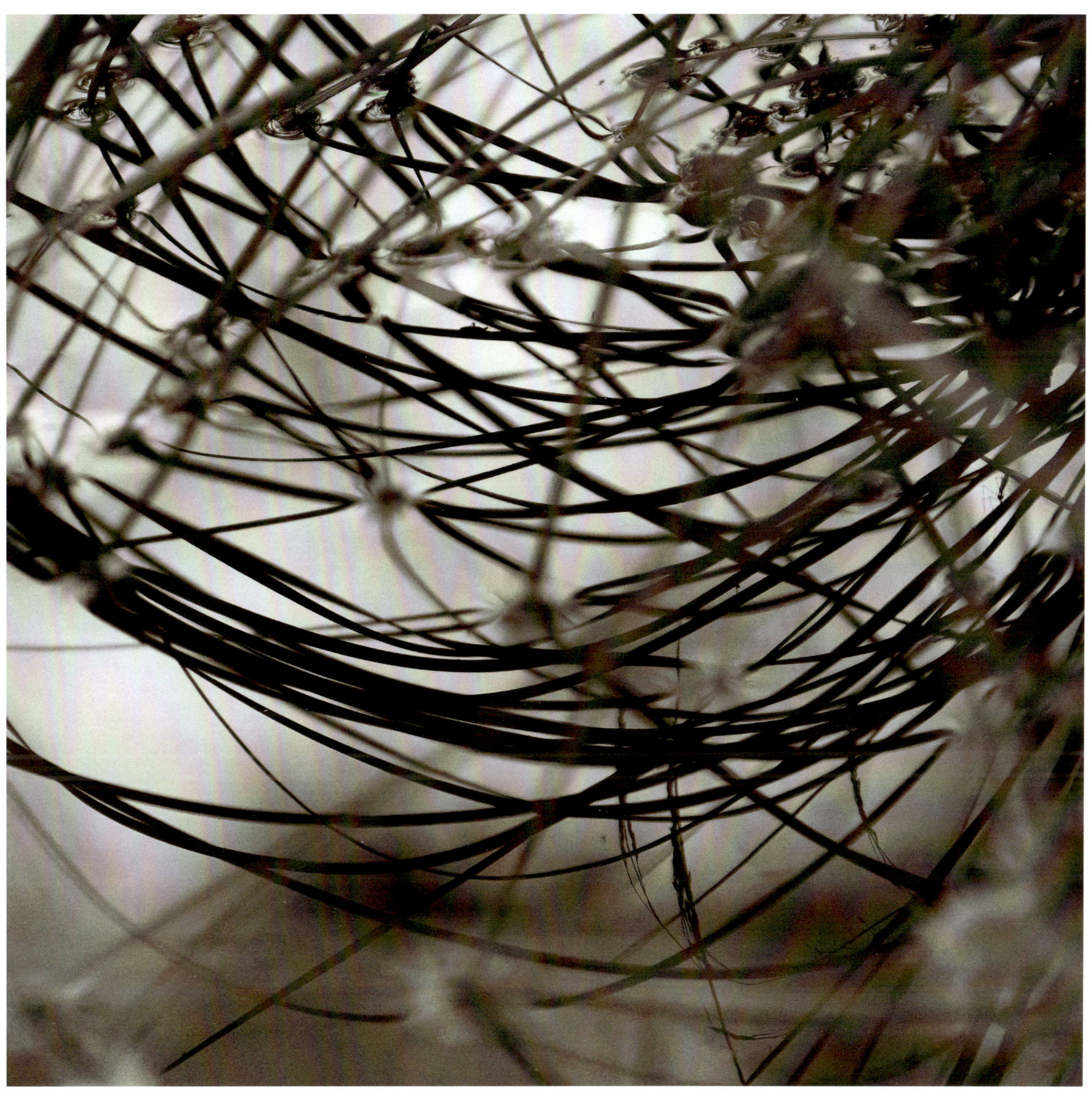

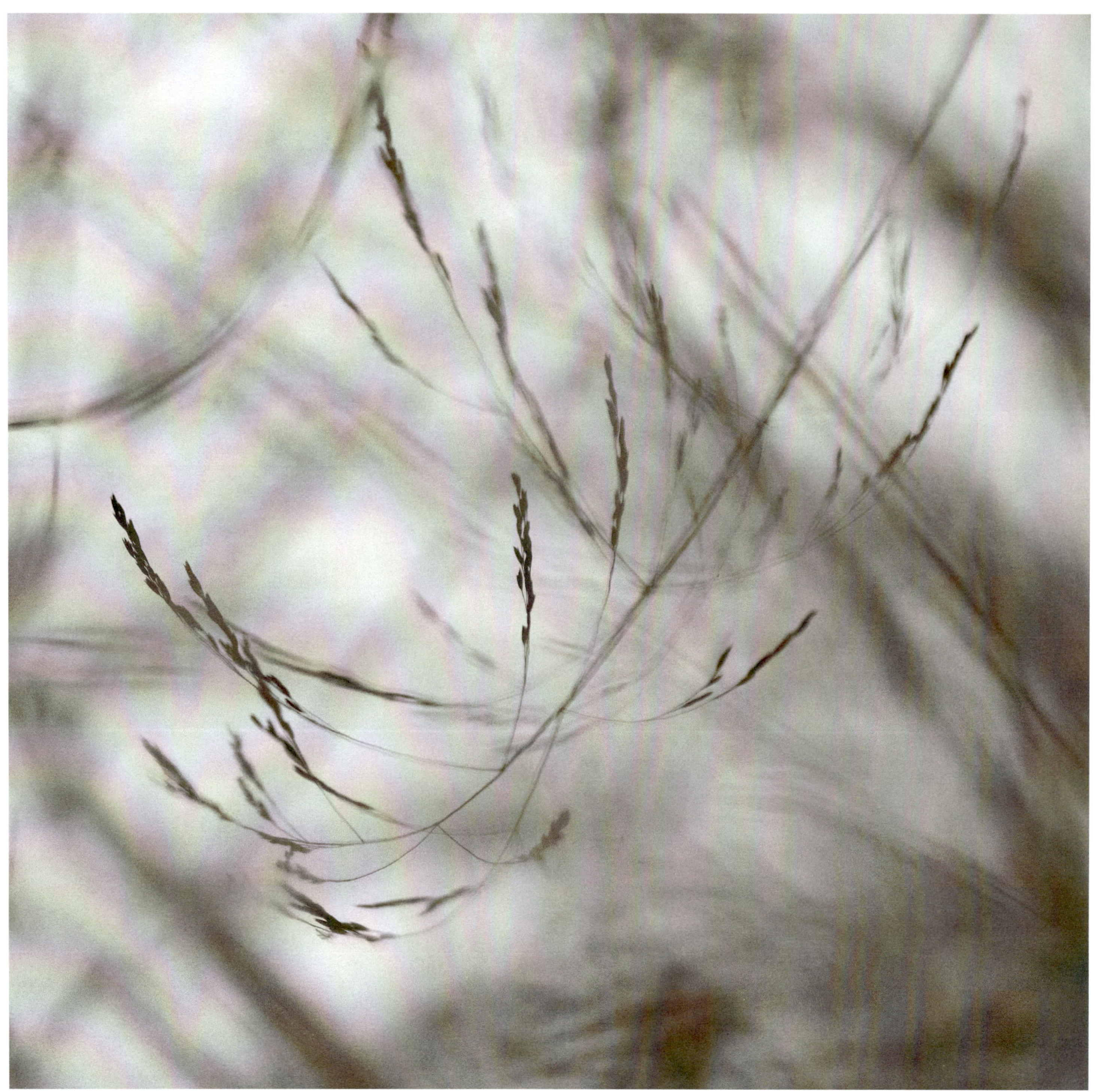

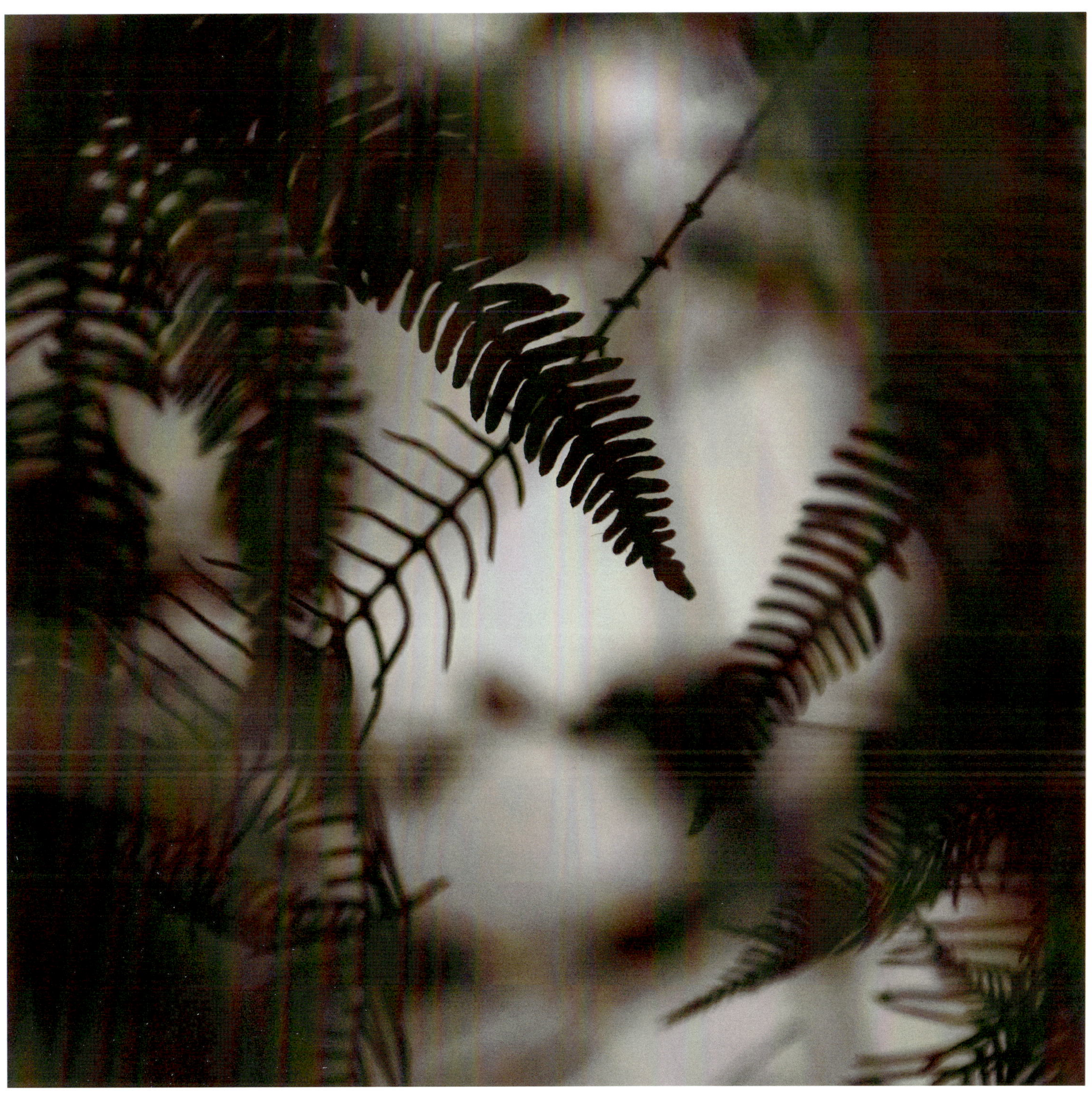

Iain Sarjeant

Iain Sarjeant is a photographer
based in the Scottish Highlands. His
photography explores both natural
and man-made environments, and
the interaction between the two. His
work is often concerned with change
– human impact on the landscape but
also the reverse, where nature regains
it's hold. He is drawn to ordinary places
– whether in an urban setting or in
his local countryside - seeking to find
interest in the common-place.